Corporate Acquis
and Mergers
in Germany

Second Edition

Corporate Acquisitions and Mergers in Germany

Second Edition

Dieter Beinert
Hengeler Mueller Weitzel Wirtz

KLUWER LAW
INTERNATIONAL

LONDON – THE HAGUE – BOSTON

Published by
Kluwer Law International Ltd
Sterling House
66 Wilton Road
London SW1V 1DE
United Kingdom

Sold and distributed
in the USA and Canada
by Kluwer Law International
675 Massachusetts Avenue
Cambridge MA 02139
USA

Kluwer Law International Ltd incorporates
the publishing programmes of
Graham & Trotman Ltd,
Kluwer Law & Taxation Publishers
and Martinus Nijhoff Publishers

In all other countries
sold and distributed by
Kluwer Law International
PO Box 322
3300 AH Dordrecht
The Netherlands

ISBN 90 411 0677 4
© Dieter Beinert, 1991, 1997
First edition 1991
Second edition 1997

The material in this book originally appeared as a chapter in *Corporate Acquisitions and Mergers* (ed. Peter Begg), a looseleaf available in two volumes from Kluwer Law International.

British Library Cataloguing in Publication Data and Library of Congress
A catalogue record for this book is available from the British Library.

Library of Congress Cataloguing-in-Publication Data is available

Typeset in Times by Selwood Systems, Midsomer Norton
Printed and bound in Great Britain by Hartnolls Ltd, Bodmin, Cornwall

Contents

I. INTRODUCTION

Germany's mergers and acquisitions market is the second largest within the European Union. The downward trend in acquisition activities which went hand in hand with the 1992/93 recession seems to have come to an end. The German economy is getting back on its feet. Experts estimate a total of some 3000 transactions involving German companies in 1996 (as opposed to some 2500 in 1995).

German companies have become attractive targets and have at the same time acquired the financial muscle to finance their own expansion plans. Corporate groups are restructuring in their move back to core business. The single European market, combined with the regeneration of Eastern Europe, have added a considerable stimulus to takeover activities. Indeed, with the establishment of market economies in Eastern Europe and East Germany's accession to the Federal Republic, entailing the extension of West German law to the whole of Germany, German companies have become even more attractive targets for foreign investors. Acquisitions of businesses in Germany will not only give direct access to Europe's largest national market, to say nothing of the whole of the single European market, but will also serve as a platform for investments in Eastern Europe.

The vast majority of the transactions to date have related to the acquisition of medium-sized, mostly family-owned, businesses, which make up the bulk of active companies in Germany. It is estimated that about 300,000 of those medium-sized companies may face problems of succession for family owners until the year 2000 and, therefore, potentially come up for sale. Medium-sized companies often turn out to be extraordinarily profitable, with correspondingly strong balance sheets, and make particularly attractive targets for that reason. Acquisitions of large companies may, of course, attract more interest from the media and public but they are essentially of less economic importance, at least so far as their effect on the German economy as a whole is concerned.

Apart from the control of mergers under the Act against Restraints of Competition, the acquisition of a business in Germany is at present not subject to any specific rules of law, nor is there any regulatory authority which supervises or enforces compliance with any general statutory provisions. The German attitude towards foreign investments is one of the most liberal in the European Union and, as such, foreign investors are likely to be agreeably surprised to find that they are hardly at a disadvantage compared to German investors.

1

II. THE CORPORATE ENVIRONMENT

1. Common Forms of Doing Business

(a) Overview

The foreign investor who wants to acquire a business or to establish a joint venture in Germany will find a somewhat puzzling variety of legal forms of business organisation. Besides the sole proprietorship (*Einzelkaufmännisches Unternehmen*), there are several types of corporations, partnerships, and other forms of enterprise. The common corporations are the limited liability company (*Gesellschaft mit beschränkter Haftung — GmbH*), the stock corporation (*Aktiengesellschaft — AG*) and the partnership limited by shares (*Kommanditgesellschaft auf Aktien — KGaA*). Partnerships may take the form of a civil law partnership (*Gesellschaft Bürgerlichen Rechts — GbR*), a general (commercial) partnership (*Offene Handelsgesellschaft — OHG*), a limited (commercial) partnership (*Kommanditgesellschaft — KG* or *GmbH & Co. KG*) or a silent partnership (*Stille Gesellschaft*). In addition to the private law companies, there are also public law corporations (*öffentliche Anstalten*) participating in business, in particular in the area of private banking and insurance. However, public law corporations by their very nature are unlikely to prove suitable targets for acquisitions.

It is difficult to determine the number and importance of the different business organisations in Germany because the relevant data are not tracked systematically. On the basis of the value added tax statistics and information available at the commercial registers, the following estimates are being made.*

In terms of numbers, most businesses in Germany are operated as sole proprietorships (more than 1.9m by the end of 1992). The vast majority of German corporations are GmbHs (amounting to some 550,000 by the end of 1992). The AG is found less frequently, although most of the large German enterprises are incorporated in this form, while the KGaA is relatively rare (their numbers amounting to approximately 3600 and 30 respectively by the end of 1994). Commercial partnerships mostly take the form of a KG or GmbH & Co. KG (some 86,000 by the end of 1992), or that of an OHG (some 210,000 by the end of 1992).

In terms of economic importance, the picture is different. Sole pro-

---

* Cf. Hansen, *Die Aktiengesellschaft 1995*, p. R228 *et seq.* and p. R272 *et seq.*

prietorships account for 15% of the sales of all businesses, commercial partnerships for almost 29% and corporations (AGs and GmbHs) for more than 50%. Fifty per cent of the aggregate sales are achieved by only 0.2% of the businesses, each of which has sales of DM100m or more. Within this sales category (DM100m or more), the different business forms are represented as follows: AGs with 98% of their aggregate sales, KGs with 50%, OHGs with 43.4%, GmbHs with 42.5% and sole proprietorships with only 2.4% (all figures as per the end of 1992).

Only the AG and the KGaA can issue stock evidenced by negotiable instruments qualifying for stock exchange listing. Interests in other corporations, such as the GmbH, as well as interests in partnerships are not appropriate for trading, do not constitute negotiable instruments, and do not qualify for listing on stock exchanges. By the end of 1994, the shares of only 810 AGs were traded at one or more of the eight German stock exchanges.

The types of business which are likely to prove interesting as investments by foreign investors will be briefly described below.

(b) Sole Proprietorship (*Einzelkaufmännisches Unternehmen*)

A sole proprietorship is an unincorporated business owned by a single natural person (entrepreneur) and operated in his name or under a trade name. The sole proprietorship is not a legal entity. It cannot have any rights and obligations of its own, nor can it sue or be sued in court. It is the owner who holds all the rights and who is fully liable for all the business debts. Depending on its size and range of activities, the sole proprietorship has to be registered in the commercial register (*Handelsregister*).

This business form is typically found in relation to small but sometimes even medium-sized enterprises. An acquisition of a sole proprietorship will customarily be effected as an asset purchase transaction, unless the owner first converts the business into a company and then sells the shares to the acquiror.

(c) Civil Law Partnership (*Gesellschaft Bürgerlichen Rechts*)

The civil law partnership (*Gesellschaft Bürgerlichen Rechts*, abbreviated as *GbR* or *BGB-Gesellschaft*) is an association of two or more natural or legal persons without corporate organisation. It is established by the execution of a partnership agreement in which the partners undertake to pursue a common purpose. The common purpose may be of any nature. However, a "full" commercial business (*vollkaufmännisches*

Handelsgewerbe) as defined in the Commercial Code can be operated only through a commercial partnership (OHG or KG) or a corporation. The BGB-Gesellschaft therefore can operate only a non-commercial, in particular non-profit-oriented business or small commercial business which does not require a commercial operation.

The BGB-Gesellschaft has no legal capacity. It is not registered in the commercial register. It cannot operate under a registered firm name nor can it acquire rights or undertake obligations. The assets of the partnership belong to its partners jointly. All partners are jointly and severally liable for partnership debts. Such liability may be limited to the partnership assets only by agreement with the third party creditor or by restrictions set out in the partnership agreement and made known to the third party creditor.

Under the statutory concept, the BGB-Gesellschaft is managed and represented jointly by all partners. However, the partnership agreement may provide otherwise. The partners are largely free to structure the partnership agreement within their discretion and according to their specific needs. Any amendment to the partnership agreement requires the unanimous consent of all partners. The partnership agreement may provide, within limits, that amendments can be made by a resolution passed by a majority of the partners.

Because of its flexibility, the BGB-Gesellschaft is suitable for a wide variety of purposes. Major construction projects are usually carried out by several construction companies which form a civil law partnership which is then called an *Arbeitsgemeinschaft* or (abbreviated) an *ARGE*. Joint research and development by several companies is quite often effected in the form of a civil law partnership.

The BGB-Gesellschaft is the basic form of partnership. All other types of partnership are variations thereof.

(d) General Partnership (*Offene Handelsgesellschaft*)

The general partnership (*Offene Handelsgesellschaft*, abbreviated as *OHG*) is a commercial partnership established by two or more natural or legal persons for the purpose of operating a "full" commercial business (*vollkaufmännisches Handelsgewerbe*) under a firm name, provided that all partners are fully liable for the partnership's debts. The OHG must be registered in the commercial register. However, it is not necessary to file the partnership agreement. The partnership agreement is therefore not subject to public inspection.

The OHG is not a legal entity separate from its partners but comes close to it. In contrast to the BGB-Gesellschaft, the OHG has a firm name under which it can carry out legal transactions. The OHG may, under its firm name, acquire rights, incur obligations and sue or be sued in court. Although the OHG has a status similar to that of a corporation in its dealings with third parties, there remain significant differences. The assets of the partnership are jointly owned by the partners. The partners are jointly and severally liable without limitation for the obligations of the partnership. Each partner is individually entitled to manage and represent the partnership, unless the partnership agreement provides otherwise.

Any amendment of the partnership agreement requires the unanimous consent of all partners. The partnership agreement may, within limits, provide otherwise.

The OHG is a business form typically used by a small number of partners who personally rely on each other and wish to commit all their assets to an undertaking. Trading companies and private banks have in the past quite frequently been organised as an OHG. More recently, the OHG has been used when businesses were reorganised for tax reasons, in particular in the leasing area. However, the overall importance of the OHG has significantly decreased and different legal forms avoiding personal liability, such as the GmbH and the GmbH & Co. KG, have increasingly been preferred.

(e) Limited Partnership (*Kommanditgesellschaft*)

The limited partnership (*Kommanditgesellschaft*, abbreviated as *KG*) is a commercial partnership established by two or more natural or legal persons for the purpose of operating a commercial business under a firm name, as is the case with the OHG. The KG is a special form of commercial partnership insofar as it is required to have two kinds of partners.

There are one or more general partners (*persönlich haftende Gesellschafter* or *Komplementäre*) having a legal status identical to that of a partner in an OHG. They manage and represent the partnership and are subject to direct unlimited and personal liability to the creditors of the partnership. In addition, there are one or more limited partners (*Kommanditisten*) whose personal liability is limited to the amount of their fixed capital contribution to the partnership. This amount is registered in the commercial register and, to the extent it has been paid into the partnership by the limited partner and not been repaid, he is discharged from personal liability. Under the statutory regime, the limited partners are excluded from the management and representation of the partnership.

The legal nature of the KG is identical to that of an OHG. The statutory provisions regulating the OHG in principle also apply to the KG. Differences in the two company forms result from the status of the limited partner. According to the statutory concept, the general partner is an entrepreneur, like the partner of an OHG, who makes his contribution by providing personal services and committing his private assets to the enterprise. The limited partner is typically an investor; he provides capital and is not involved in the management of the business. However, since most provisions of the law on partnerships are not mandatory, this difference may be wiped out almost entirely by the partnership agreement.

Any amendment to the partnership agreement requires the unanimous consent of all partners, unless the partnership agreement provides otherwise.

The economic significance of the KG has steadily increased during the last decades. This company form is frequently used for family-owned enterprises. Quite often it has been employed for bringing together capital from investors for particular ventures. The KG is particularly popular in a form in which the sole general partner is a corporation, typically, a GmbH. It is safe to say that the KG, together with the GmbH, represents one of the most frequent forms of business organisation found in Germany.

(f) GmbH & Co. KG

A commercial partnership may have corporate partners, such as a GmbH or an AG. A corporation which is a partner in an OHG or a general partner in a KG is, like any other general partner, fully liable to the creditors of the partnership. However, under the principles of corporate law, only the corporation as such (and not the shareholders of the corporation) is liable for its obligations.

A frequently encountered combination of the commercial partnership and the corporation is that of a KG in which the only general partner is a GmbH (the so-called *GmbH & Co. KG*). In its typical form, the shares in the GmbH are held exclusively by the limited partners of the KG and the percentage of their shareholding in the GmbH is equal to their interests in the KG. The GmbH commonly has no equity interest in the KG but is entitled only to some small compensation (e.g. 5% per annum of its share capital) for the assumption of personal liability and reimbursement of expenditures. The share capital of the

GmbH often does not exceed the statutory minimum of DM50,000.

Although the GmbH & Co. KG comes close to a corporation, it is recognised under commercial law, and in principle also under tax law, as a partnership. Its popularity results from the fact that it combines the advantages of a partnership with those of a corporation, which may outweigh the disadvantages resulting from a somewhat complex corporate structure. It provides the overall limitation of liability subsisting in a corporation and has the flexible structure of a partnership. In general, it is taxed as a partnership, which gives certain advantages over the taxation of a corporation (e.g. direct accrual of profits and losses to the partners). On the other hand, tax benefits can be gained by making the limited partners employees of the GmbH.

In a few instances, the GmbH & Co. KG serves as a tool to avoid co-determination under the 1976 Co-Determination Act (*Mitbestimmungsgesetz*), pursuant to which a corporation (but not a commercial partnership) having regularly more than 2000 employees must establish a supervisory board composed equally of owner representatives and employees (see p. 129 below). However, under s 4 of the Co-Determination Act, the employees of the KG are generally considered as employees of the GmbH for purposes of the applicability of the law if the majority of the limited partners in the KG also holds the majority in the GmbH.

The GmbH & Co. KG may also help to escape disclosure requirements with regard to financial statements under the Commercial Code because the disclosure obligations under s 325 *et seq.* of the Commercial Code (so far) apply only to corporations. However, strong attempts are being made by the EU Commission to treat the GmbH & Co. KG as a corporation for disclosure purposes. The EC Directive dated 8th November 1990 provides that partnerships which have only corporations as unlimited liable partners shall be subject to the Fourth and Seventh EC Directives on the Harmonisation of Company Law. The implementation of this Directive into German law, which is overdue but nontheless not treated with priority by the German legislature, would make the GmbH & Co. KG subject to the same disclosure requirements as a corporation. A large GmbH & Co. KG, however, would be subject to disclosure requirements under the Disclosure Act (*Publizitätsgesetz*).

Finally, the GmbH & Co. KG is sometimes used for joint ventures between German and foreign investors when the German investors are interested in a direct accrual of profits and losses whereas the foreign investors wish to use a German corporate subsidiary to participate in the joint venture.

(g) **Silent Partnership** (*Stille Gesellschaft*)

The silent partnership is a partnership in which the silent partner participates in the commercial business of the active partner by making a capital contribution. The contribution becomes part of the active partner's business assets and the silent partner participates in the profits and losses of the business. The silent partner may contract out of his participation in the losses whereas his participation in the profits is mandatory.

The silent partnership is a specific form of civil law partnership. It is not a legal entity and it possesses no assets. The partnership is of an internal nature only. It is neither registered in the commercial register nor is it otherwise apparent to the public. Only the active partner acquires rights and assumes obligations under transactions with third parties. The silent partner is not liable for any debts of the enterprise in which he invests.

In a *typical* silent partnership, the silent partner's position is comparable to that of a lender. He makes a capital contribution and, instead of receiving fixed interest, he participates in the profits (and losses) of the business. The capital contribution qualifies as debt rather than equity. This is why a typical silent partnership is treated as a loan for tax purposes. Where the silent partnership is structured in such a way that the silent partner not only participates in profits and losses but also in the assets of the business, in particular in the accrued unrealised gain, the goodwill and the liquidation surplus, the partnership qualifies as a so-called *atypical* silent partnership and the silent partner is treated for tax purposes as a partner in an ordinary commercial limited partnership having business income.

The silent partnership is frequently used for financing and investment purposes. It permits capitalisation without creating any personal liability on the part of the investor and without involving public disclosure. Foreign investors can gain substantial tax advantages when financing a German corporation in which they hold an interest through a typical silent partnership rather than through equity, because profits distributed to the silent partner constitute a deductible business expense for the German corporation for corporate income tax purposes. However, for trade tax purposes, the contribution by a foreign silent partner is treated as equity. While the silent partner's profit share is subject to withholding tax under internal law, a foreign recipient may be exempt from withholding under an applicable tax treaty. This financing method has been restricted, however, by s 8a of the Corporate Income Tax Act (see p. 103 *et seq.* below). An atypical silent partnership is normally not desirable for a foreign investor because it results in the creation of a taxable permanent establishment.

(h) Limited Liability Company
(*Gesellschaft mit beschränkter Haftung*)

The limited liability company (*Gesellschaft mit beschränkter Haftung*, abbreviated as *GmbH*) is the most common form of incorporation in Germany. It is designed to be used as a closely held or private corporation. The Act governing the GmbH (*GmbH-Gesetz*) is relatively brief and affords the shareholders a substantial degree of flexibility.

A GmbH may be established by one or more shareholders who may be natural or legal persons. The minimum share capital is DM50,000. The GmbH comes into legal existence upon registration in the commercial register.

The GmbH is a legal entity separate from its shareholders. It may acquire its own rights and incur its own obligations and it may sue and be sued in court. The liability of its shareholders is limited to the amount of their subscription to the share capital. Once incorporated and registered in the commercial register and once the share capital contribution subscribed for has been made (and not repaid), the shareholders have no further liability, unless the articles of association provide otherwise or the shareholders have assumed personal obligations. However, it is important to be aware that each shareholder is liable for the share capital contributions of all other shareholders, though this liability is only secondary. Beyond that, the personal liability of shareholders arises only in exceptional cases where the corporate veil is pierced (see p. 21 *et seq.* below).

The GmbH must have one or more managing directors (*Geschäftsführer*) who manage and represent the company. The managing directors may, generally speaking, be removed at any time, notwithstanding the fact that their employment contracts remain in force and will therefore have to be honoured. Limitations on the statutory authority of the managing directors to bind the company contractually have no effect with respect to third parties.

The supreme authority in the company lies with the shareholders' meeting. The shareholders decide (for example) on any amendment to the articles of association, including capital increases and reductions. They approve the annual financial statements and resolve on the distribution of profits. They decide on the appointment and removal of managing directors and members of the supervisory board, if any.*

It is not only issues of an extraordinary nature which are subject to the approval of the shareholders. The shareholders can give binding instructions to the managing directors with regard to all company matters, even so far as the day-to-day business of the company is concerned. The articles of association can limit or extend the authority of the shareholders. In practice, the articles often specify business transactions for which the managing directors internally require the prior approval of the shareholders.

Shareholders' resolutions are, in general, passed by a simple majority of the votes cast, unless the articles of association provide otherwise. For particularly important resolutions, such as amendments to the articles of association, capital increases or reductions and mergers, the law requires a majority of three quarters of the votes cast (though the articles may require an even larger majority). A shareholder holding more than 25% of the capital can block these key resolutions (*Sperrminorität* — blocking minority). An increase in the obligations of the shareholders can be resolved only with the consent of all shareholders.

As a rule, the GmbH has a one-tier structure, composed only of the managing directors. However, the articles of association can always provide for a supervisory board, thus establishing a two-tier structure. The shareholders are largely free to structure the composition and functions of such an optional supervisory board as they wish. An optional board may be given the right to supervise the managing directors. Most of the powers vested in the shareholders' meeting may be conferred on the board (e.g. prior approval of certain transactions, appointment and removal of managing directors).

A GmbH which has more than 500 employees is subject to employee co-determination. Such a GmbH must have a supervisory board in which employees are represented. The level of employee representation as well as the rights and obligations of the mandatory supervisory board depend on which of the four co-determination acts is applicable (see pp. 129–130 below).

The GmbH Act does not require the issue of share certificates. The articles of association may provide that share certificates be issued but

---

* Except insofar as co-determination laws require members to be employee-elected. See pp. 129–130 below.

rarely do so in practice. Even if share certificates are issued, they are not in any case capable of serving as negotiable instruments. Shares in a GmbH can be transferred only by an assignment effected in notarial form. The articles may require that share certificates be delivered in addition.

Ownership of shares is not entered in the commercial register. The GmbH only has to file a list of its shareholders on an annual basis with the commercial register and to notify the commercial register when all the shares of the company have come under the control of a single shareholder. Moreover, there is no statutory requirement for the company to maintain a share register or ledger identifying the owners of shares, nor is it typical for a GmbH to keep such records on a voluntary basis. On the other hand, a well-managed company may reasonably be expected to keep so-called company files which evidence the ownership of shares on a voluntary basis. Where no such files are kept in an orderly fashion, it may be difficult in an acquisition to identify the true owners of shares.

The shares in a GmbH cannot be listed on a stock exchange. Nevertheless, the GmbH clearly plays a dominant role in German business life. Due to its simplicity both in formation and operation and its adaptability to various shareholders' needs, the GmbH has become the most popular corporate form, and is also much favoured by foreign investors. As a result, the GmbH is the most common acquisition target in Germany. By the end of 1992, there were about 550,000 GmbHs, with an aggregate share capital of around DM246bn. Although the great majority of GmbHs are small or medium-sized, there is a substantial number of GmbHs which are comparable in size to some of the large AGs.

(i) **Stock Corporation** (*Aktiengesellschaft*)

The stock corporation (*Aktiengesellschaft*, abbreviated as *AG*) is the form of incorporation traditionally used for large publicly held enterprises. Its shares may be listed and traded in the stock market. The AG is governed by the Stock Corporation Act (*Aktiengesetz*), a rather comprehensive statute providing for detailed, complex and mostly mandatory rules on the establishment and operation of the corporation.

(1) *Establishment*
The establishment of an AG requires one or more incorporators who may be natural persons or legal entities. The minimum share capital is DM100,000. The AG comes into legal existence upon entry in the commercial register. Like the GmbH, the AG is a legal entity separate

from its shareholders. However unlike the GmbH, the AG has a mandatory two-tier system, a management board (*Vorstand*) and a supervisory board (*Aufsichtsrat*). The responsibilities of both boards are strictly segregated and it is not permissible to serve on both boards at the same time.

(2) *Management Board*

The management board (*Vorstand*) may be composed of one or several members. The usual practice is to have a management board with several members and to appoint one member as chairman (*Vorsitzender*) or speaker (*Sprecher*). The management board manages and represents the company. The management authority of the management board is very broad, ranging from day-to-day management to fundamental corporate policy and strategy decisions and the implementation thereof. The board's authority to commit the company vis-à-vis third parties cannot be restricted. Internal restrictions on the management authority may be imposed, but to a far lesser extent than in a GmbH. In particular, neither the shareholders' meeting, nor the supervisory board have any authority to give instructions to the management board. In fact, the subjection of the management board to instructions by a controlling shareholder or to any other corporate influence may even result in a liability to compensate the company for disadvantages suffered thereby.

A right of a shareholder to give the management board instructions may only be created by a so-called control agreement (*Beherrschungsvertrag*) in accordance with s 291 *et seq.* of the Stock Corporation Act. A control agreement has to be entered into between the controlling shareholder and the controlled company and requires the consent by the share-holders' meeting of the controlled company. The major drawbacks of such an agreement are that it has to provide for the annual compensation by the controlling shareholder of any losses suffered by the controlled company during the term of the agreement (whether or not such losses were caused by instructions of the controlling shareholder), and that it has to provide in favour of all outside shareholders (i.e. all shareholders other than the controlling shareholder) both for a guaranteed annual dividend and for appraisal rights.

The sweeping statutory authorities of the management board have been restricted during the last years. The Federal Supreme Court held in a landmark case in 1982 that the management board is required to obtain the prior approval of the shareholders' meeting in all cases where the board wants to carry out a decision which has such a significant impact on the company or the rights and interests of its shareholders that the board cannot reasonably assume that it is entitled to take such decision exclusively in its own responsibility.* This decision resulted in considerable uncertainty as to its consequences but it was the starting point for a clear trend to impose limitations on the authority of the management board, in particular in the cases of major acquisitions, divestitures and reorganisations.

The members of the management board are appointed and removed by the supervisory board. They cannot be appointed for a term of office of more than five years. Five-year terms are customary; renewed appointments are permissible. During their term of office, the members of the management board cannot be removed, except for cause. Cause is deemed to exist, *inter alia*, when the shareholders' meeting withdraws its confidence for reasons which are not manifestly arbitrary. Broad management authority and protection against removal during their term of office, reinforced by the protection granted to members of the supervisory board mentioned below, afford the members of the management board in an AG a much stronger position and substantially more independence than is available to managing directors in a GmbH. This relatively firm and independent position of the management board is one of several reasons why hostile takeovers may appear less attractive in Germany than in other jurisdictions.

(3) *Supervisory Board*
The supervisory board (*Aufsichtsrat*) is composed of at least three members. Depending on the amount of the share capital, the articles may provide for up to 21 members. Subject to the applicable co-determination law (see p. 129 below), up to 50% of the board members must be employee-elected. The other members, i.e. shareholder representatives, are appointed and removed by the shareholders. The shareholder-appointed members are either elected by the shareholders' meeting or, if the articles so provide, designated by individual shareholders. Quite frequently, many of the shareholder representatives are experienced outsiders, such as bankers or top executives from other companies. The members of the supervisory board are not subject to any instructions.

In practice the term of office for members of the supervisory board is, as a rule, about five years, which is equal to the statutory maximum. Renewed appointments are permissible. Prior to the expiration of their term of office, members elected by the shareholders' meeting may be

---

* Federal Supreme Court, decision of 25th February 1982, BGHZ 83, 122 ("*Holzmüller*").
  The most important and valuable business of the company was transferred to a newly established subsidiary outside the direct control of the shareholders.

removed at any time by shareholders' resolution. However, such resolutions generally require a majority of three quarters of the votes cast. Shareholder-designated members may be removed and replaced at any time by the shareholder entitled to the nomination right. Employee-elected members can be removed only in accordance with the applicable co-determination law or, if there is good cause, by the court.

The main function of the supervisory board is to appoint and supervise the members of the management board. The supervisory board has no management functions. It may give recommendations but no instructions to the management board. Even in the case of extraordinary transactions the management board does not need the prior approval of the supervisory board, unless the supervisory board itself or the articles of association have defined certain transactions as requiring such prior approval. If prior approval is required but denied by the supervisory board, the management board may refer the matter to the shareholders' meeting, which can overrule the supervisory board with a majority of three-quarters of the votes cast.

In order to enable the supervisory board to carry out its functions, it has been empowered with broad information rights. In particular, the management board shall regularly report to the supervisory board on the intended business policy and other basic questions of management, as well as on the profitability of the company, the development of business and transactions which may be of substantial importance for the profitability or liquidity of the company. The supervisory board may at any time request that the management board deliver a report on specific corporate matters.

The institution of the supervisory board has become the target of increasing criticism. During the last years well-known German companies have suffered considerable losses which were attributed, at least in part, to inadequate control over management by the supervisory board. It is not likely that these incidents will result in a major overhaul of Germany's system of corporate governance, as it has been suggested, but they will certainly fuel the trend towards restricting the freedom of management and making it more accountable to both the supervisory board and the shareholders' meeting. Also, there is growing agreement that the supervisory board should be "professionalised", in particular by installing a full-time chairman, and that the number of supervisory board positions a person can hold at the same time should be reduced substantially below the currently applicable threshold of 10.

(4) Shareholders' Meeting

The powers of the shareholders' meeting (*Hauptversammlung*) are relatively limited, particularly if compared with the powers of shareholders of a GmbH. The main responsibilities of that meeting consist of the election of the supervisory board members (except insofar as they are designated by individual shareholders or elected by the employees in accordance with the applicable co-determination law), the application of the profits, the appointment of auditors and amendments to the articles, including increases and reductions of share capital. Furthermore, its consent is required for the execution of certain corporate agreements (e.g. control agreements — *Beherrschungsverträge*, profit transfer agreements — *Gewinnabführungsverträge*), and for certain corporate measures substantially affecting the company, such as mergers, changes of legal form, the disposal of all of the assets of the AG and similar measures. The shareholders' meeting may not give instructions to the management board. Only upon the express request of the management board may it decide on management issues. This adds substantially to the independence enjoyed by members of the management board.

Shareholders' resolutions require a majority of the votes cast, unless the Stock Corporation Act or the articles of association provide for a larger majority or other requirements. Certain important resolutions require, in addition to the simple majority of the votes cast, a majority of three quarters of the capital participating in the vote. This is true for all amendments to the articles of association and for other important resolutions, such as changes of the share capital, the issue of convertible bonds, corporate agreements and mergers. The articles of association may provide, within limits, for different (mostly larger) majorities and for additional requirements. The holding of more than one quarter of the share capital is therefore often referred to as a blocking minority (*Sperrminorität*).

(5) Shares and Voting Rights

The shares in an AG may be bearer shares (*Inhaberaktien*) or registered shares (*Namensaktien*). In most cases, the shares are bearer shares. It is also common practice to issue share certificates. Both types of shares are negotiable instruments and can be listed and traded on stock exchanges. The shares are freely transferable. While the transfer of bearer shares requires no registration, the transfer of registered shares must be notified to the AG and registered in its stock ledger. Only a person registered in the stock ledger is recognised as a shareholder by the AG.

The articles may provide that a transfer of registered shares requires the consent of the AG in order to be valid (so-called restricted registered shares — *vinkulierte Namensaktien*). Consent is given by the management board, unless the articles confer this right on the supervisory board or the shareholders' meeting. The articles may set out grounds on which the consent can be denied. The requirement of consent for the transfer of shares is a means of retaining control over the composition of the shareholders which is often applied within family or closely held companies, but which may also be used as protection against foreign investors.

Shares must be stated in fixed nominal amounts of Deutsche marks. The minimum amount has been reduced in 1994 from DM50 to DM5. Shares without par value are not permitted.

Generally, each share confers the right to vote and the number of votes attached to a share is determined by the par value thereof. There can be shares of different classes affording different rights, in particular with regard to dividends. Besides the ordinary or common shares, so-called preferred shares (*Vorzugsaktien*) with or without voting rights may be issued. Non-voting preferred shares may be issued only with a cumulative preference as to dividends and their aggregate par value must not exceed the aggregate par value of the voting shares. Shares with multiple voting rights are generally not permissible. Limitations on the voting rights attached to the shares held by one shareholder to a certain ceiling (e.g. to 5% of the aggregate share capital) may be imposed by the articles, however. A considerable number of major AGs have provided for such a limitation. However, more recently there is a tendency to restrict attempts to limit voting rights and to return to the principle of "one share, one vote." In any case, a limitation of voting rights is disregarded for purposes of calculating the majority of capital in cases where resolutions require a majority of the capital participating therein.

(6) *Some Numbers*
The number of AGs existing in Germany is relatively small and the German stock market is very narrow. There were only about 3600 AGs at the end of 1994. By the end of 1994 the shares of only 810 AGs were traded on one of the German stock exchanges.* Only about 150 shares are actively traded and the sales in the six most actively traded shares represent more than 50% of the total stock exchange

---

* In comparison: by such date 7684 domestic corporations were listed in the USA (NYSE: 2353; Amex: 751; NASDAQ: 4580); 2888 in Japan and 1803 in Great Britain/Ireland.

turnover in Germany. The aggregate market value of all listed AGs amounted to DM774bn at the end of 1994.*

The form of the AG is typically chosen by large companies which wish to attract funds from numerous persons, particularly through the stock markets. During recent years there has been a tendency to convert medium-sized and family-owned businesses into AGs and have their shares listed on the stock exchanges. This trend towards "going public" has not so far laid the ground for a substantial increase in takeover activities. While some of the newcomers turned out not to be as attractive as first anticipated, others had only their non-voting preferred shares publicly traded and kept a close hold on the voting shares. Although it is estimated that there are some 2000 potential candidates for going public in the medium term, the present reality is still different. During the three-year period from 1993 to 1995 a mere 40 AGs had their shares listed in Germany.

(7) *New Law on Small Stock Corporations*
In the second half of 1994 the Act on Small Stock Corporations and for the Deregulation of the Stock Corporation Act was adopted (*Gesetz für kleine Aktiengesellschaften und zur Deregulierung des Aktienrechts* of 2nd August 1994.)

It is the primary goal of the law to make the AG more attractive for smaller and medium-sized enterprises which have traditionally been organised as GmbHs or commercial partnerships. The law provides for a number of reliefs for closely-held, typically non-listed stock corporations. For instance, it requires only one incorporator for the establishment of the company, it allows the company more flexibility with regard to profit appropriation and it eases some formalities with regard to shareholders' meetings. Furthermore, it places an AG which has been established after 10th August 1994 and has less than 500 employees on equal footing with a GmbH of the same size in so far as such an AG shall no longer be subject to co-determination on the supervisory board level. It is hoped that, once more businesses will have chosen the legal form of an AG, there will be a stronger movement towards "going public".

Another important element of the new law — which is in fact designed for large companies — is the attempt to facilitate equity financing by the issuance of shares. The new law makes it considerably easier to exclude the statutory pre-emptive right of shareholders (*Bezugsrechte*) in

---

* The respective figures were for the USA DM7772bn, for Japan DM10243bn and for Great Britain/Ireland DM1806bn.

case of capital increases. An exclusion of the statutory pre-emptive right is deemed permissible if the offering price for the new shares is not substantially below the current stock exchange price and if the capital increase does not exceed 10% of the company's registered share capital.

(j) Partnership Limited by Shares
(*Kommanditgesellschaft auf Aktien*)

The partnership limited by shares (*Kommanditgesellschaft auf Aktien*, abbreviated as *KGaA*) is a corporate form which combines the form of an AG with elements of a limited partnership. There must be one or more general partners who are personally liable for the debts of the company (*persönlich haftende Gesellschafter*) whereas the other members are shareholders who hold an interest in the share capital but are not personally liable for the company's debts.

The KGaA has no board of management, but is managed and represented by its general partners. It is of little commercial importance, there being only about 30 KGaAs known in Germany.

2. Majority Rights and Minority Protection

(a) Majority Rights

Any purchaser acquiring less than 100% in a company will be interested to know what rights are attributed to its level of participation and what rights are given to the remaining shareholders and partners respectively. This will be particularly true for a purchaser who considers himself not as a passive investor but as a participant who intends to exercise entrepreneurial influence. It is crucial to note that the scope of the rights and influence attributed to a participation in a company does not necessarily depend on the percentage of the capital acquired. As important are the legal form of the company concerned and, in particular, the provisions of its articles or the partnership agreement, as the case may be.

Shareholders' resolutions in *corporations* are passed by majority vote. As a rule, a simple majority (more than 50%) is sufficient. For particularly important resolutions, the law requires a qualified majority. A qualified majority is typically a majority of 75% which is necessary, for example, for amendments to the articles, increases and reductions of the share capital, mergers or the liquidation of the company. The articles may provide, within limits, for different (mostly larger) majorities and for additional requirements. Moreover, the articles may allocate, again within limits, the voting powers on a different basis from the participation in the share capital. They may (in the case of a GmbH) provide that a shareholder will always have a certain percentage of the votes (say, 51 or 75%) irrespective of his percentage of the share capital, or (in the case of both a GmbH and an AG) that the votes of any one shareholder shall not exceed a certain percentage (say, 10 or 20%), even if his percentage of the share capital is higher. However, whereas in a GmbH the supreme authority lies with the shareholders' meeting, the powers of the shareholders' meeting in an AG are relatively limited. A simple majority of 51% in a GmbH typically gives substantially more influence than the same level of participation in an AG.

As far as *partnerships* are concerned, the statutory principle is that partners' resolutions are passed unanimously. This also holds true of amendments to the partnership agreement. The partnership agreement may provide, however, that specific resolutions, including defined amendments to the partnership agreement, are made by simple majority of the votes cast. The majority may be calculated in proportion to the number of partners or to their capital contributions. The voting rights may also be allocated in such a way that they do not correspond to the percentage of the capital held. The amount of entrepreneurial influence a partner can exercise will largely depend on the provisions of the partnership agreement. In an OHG, all partners, irrespective of their equity interest, are entitled to manage and represent the company; but the partnership agreement may provide otherwise and may, for example, exclude certain partners from management and representation, or grant such authority exclusively to specified partners. A KG, according to the law, is managed and represented by its general partners, whereas the limited partners merely have rights of control, even if their capital participation exceeds the capital participation of the general partners. Sometimes the rights of control are limited by the partnership agreement merely to receiving a copy of the auditor's report on the balance sheet. On the other hand, the partnership agreement may reverse the statutory concept and give the limited partners, or some of them, a say in the company.

(b) Minority Protection

Where company issues are decided by the majority of the shareholders or partners, the minority needs to be protected. Minority protection is accomplished by different legal principles of which the more important ones are described below.

The principle of equal treatment (*Gleichbehandlungsgrundsatz*) requires that no shareholder or partner should arbitrarily be treated differently from other shareholders or partners, unless he gives his consent thereto. This principle has been enacted in s 53a of the Stock Corporation Act but constitutes a general rule of law applicable to all forms of company. It may give rise to claims by minority shareholders or partners, for example, to participate in a capital increase resolved by the majority, and it may afford minority shareholders or partners protective rights, e.g. against the granting of special rights and privileges to other shareholders or partners or against the discriminatory imposition of special duties or disadvantages.

Each shareholder and partner has fiduciary duties (*Treuepflichten*), both to the company and to the other shareholders or partners, as the case may be. These fiduciary duties impose limits on the power of the majority. Voting rights must not be exercised in an abusive manner without regard to the legitimate interests of the company and of the other shareholders or partners (see p. 23).

Each shareholder and partner has a right of information (*Informationsrecht*) with regard to company matters. A partner of an OHG and a general partner of a KG can personally inform himself of the affairs of the company, inspect its books and records and draw up accounts therefrom. A limited partner of a KG, however, may as a rule only examine the annual accounts. A shareholder of an AG can request that he be given information at a shareholders' meeting by the board of management regarding any matters of the corporation to the extent that this is necessary to evaluate any topics on the agenda; the duty to inform extends also to the legal and business relations of the corporation with affiliated enterprises. Information given to a shareholder of an AG outside a shareholders' meeting must generally, upon request, also be given within the shareholders' meeting, even if it is not related to a subject matter on the agenda. Each shareholder of a GmbH is entitled to inspect the books and records of the company and to be informed of its affairs by the managing directors.

There are a number of technical minority rights the exercise of which requires a certain quorum. For example, shareholders in an AG whose shares amount to at least 5% of the share capital of the company can request that a shareholders' meeting be held. Shareholders in an AG whose shares amount to at least 5% of the share capital or DM1m can also request that topics be put on the agenda for resolution by the shareholders. Shareholders in a GmbH whose shares amount to at least 10% of the share capital have the same rights.

Furthermore, protection of the minority is achieved by the degree of majority approval required for important decisions, by the general prohibition against voting in situations involving a conflict of interest and by the rule that management has to employ the diligence of an orderly businessman in matters relating to the company (which means, amongst other things, that management owes its loyalty to the company and not to the majority).

Finally, any shareholder, regardless of the number of shares held, may file a lawsuit to have a shareholders' resolution declared void or invalidated by the court on the grounds that it violates the law or the articles of association of the company. In particular this latter right, in combination with the right of information, has proved to be a formidable platform for increased shareholder activism. Institutional investors, associations of small shareholders and some individual "professional" shareholders have used these rights aggressively and have achieved considerable improvements as far as information policy towards shareholders, transparency of corporate matters and protection of minority shareholders in general are concerned. The drawback of this increased shareholder influence was a significant number of cases where nuisance shareholders abused their rights by blocking the implementation of important corporate decisions (e.g. mergers) and giving up their resistance only against payment of handsome amounts of money which were euphemistically declared as compensation for legal fees and expenses. In cases of obvious abuse, such payments may be recovered from the recipient, though.

3. Shareholder Liability and Piercing the Corporate Veil

The corporation is a legal entity designed to shield its owners from individual liability for its debts. As a rule, the shareholders of an AG or GmbH may enjoy this privilege of corporate protection and do not become liable for anything beyond the amount of their subscription to the share capital or the price of their shares. There are various exceptions to this principle, however, where additional liability is imposed on shareholders and where even the corporate veil may be pierced. The more important cases of shareholder liability are the following:

(a) Pre-Incorporation Liability

An AG or GmbH comes into legal existence as a corporation only upon its registration in the commercial register. However, as soon as the articles of association have been formally adopted, the company, although not yet a legal entity, may already operate its business, own assets, acquire rights and incur obligations. It is a matter of dispute whether and to what extent shareholders may become personally liable for liabilities incurred by the company during this pre-incorporation period. In any case, if the company suffers losses during the pre-incorporation period which reduce the value of the company's net assets at the time of registration below its registered share capital, then all shareholders are liable to pay the shortfall to the company in proportion to their shares (Federal Supreme Court, decision of 9th March 1981, BGHZ 80, 129).

(b) Capital Contributions, Repayment of Capital

Each shareholder of a GmbH is liable for all outstanding capital contributions of all other shareholders (GmbH Act, s 24). It does not make any difference in this context whether an outstanding capital contribution was promised at the establishment of the GmbH or on the occasion of a later capital increase. If non-cash capital contributions have been made and the true value of these contributions falls short of the stated amount of share capital to be covered by them, such liability even extends to the shortfall. The liability for outstanding capital contributions is only secondary, though.

No comparable liability exists for shareholders of an AG. An AG has typically a larger number of shareholders where such liability would be inappropriate. The statutory concept of the Stock Corporation Act is by and large designed to avoid that capital contributions remain outstanding.

Statutory law mandates that the capital of a corporation be preserved. The applicable rules vary depending on whether the corporation concerned is an AG or a GmbH (see pp. 91–92 below). Payments made or benefits granted by a corporation to its shareholders in violation of the applicable capital preservation rules have to be returned by the recipients.

(c) Contractual, Pre-Contractual and Tort Liability

Shareholder liability may arise where some or all of the shareholders assume contractual obligations towards the company or its creditors, e.g. by entering into guarantee agreements or by issuing comfort letters in favour of the company. Shareholders may also become subject to a pre-contractual liability towards third parties if, for instance, they get involved in contract negotiations between the company and a third party and such third party enters into the contract with the company in reliance on incorrect or misleading representations made by the shareholders. In exceptional cases, such as fraudulent abuses of the corporate shield, shareholders may even become liable to the company's creditors in tort.

(d) Breach of a Fiduciary Duty

A shareholder owes certain fiduciary duties (*Treuepflichten*) both to the company and his fellow shareholders (Federal Supreme Court, decision of 5th June 1975, BGHZ 65, 15 ("*ITT*"), decision of 1st February 1988, BGHZ 103, 184 ("*Linotype*") and decision of 20th March 1995, BGHZ 129, 136 ("*Girmes*")). The scope of these duties and the specific obligations resulting therefrom depend on the structure of the corporation and on the shareholder's level of participation. Depending on the circumstances, fiduciary duties may require, for instance, a majority shareholder to refrain from competition or from taking advantage of corporate opportunities. A shareholder who breaches his fiduciary duty may, among other consequences, be liable for damages suffered by the company or other shareholders.

(e) Commingling of Assets, Undercapitalisation

Shareholder liability for the company's debts may be asserted when the assets of the company and a shareholder are commingled and this is disguised by non-transparent bookkeeping or otherwise, or in cases of gross undercapitalisation when the company's registered capital is evidently insufficient to meet its financial needs (Federal Supreme Court, decision of 13th April 1994, WM 1994, 896; Federal Supreme Court, decision of 30th November 1978, NJW 1979, 2104). The courts are in general quite reluctant, however, to pierce the corporate veil, in particular vis-à-vis minority shareholders.

(f) Exercise of Controlling Influence

The legislator and the courts have used shareholder liability as a tool to protect a company and its creditors against disadvantages that may result from the exercise of a controlling influence over the company by another enterprise. In this context, not only corporations or part-nerships are considered as "enterprises" but also individuals who are engaged in other business activities.

(1) *Control Agreements**

An enterprise that has entered into a control agreement (*Beherrschungsvertrag*) with a corporation (AG or GmbH) is authorised to manage and control such corporation and give it even disadvantageous instructions. The downside of this authority is that mandatory law requires the controlling enterprise to compensate the controlled corporation for any annual net loss (*Jahresfehlbetrag*) incurred during the existence of the agreement (Stock Corporation Act, ss 302, 303 — these provisions are applied by way of analogy also to GmbHs). With regard to an AG, the control agreement must provide furthermore in favour of its outstanding shareholders both for a guaranteed annual dividend and appraisal rights (Stock Corporation Act, s 304, 305). Whether the outstanding shareholders of a GmbH are protected in the same way has not yet been decided by the courts.

(2) *Factual Control Situations*

In cases where no control agreement exists, a shareholder may factually be able to direct or influence the management or specific activities of a corporation. Such a shareholder may give priority to its own interests over the interests of the corporation and cause disadvantages or damage to the corporation.

An AG is protected against such undue influence in various ways. If a controlling enterprise influences an AG to do or not to do anything and this results in a disadvantage for the controlled AG, the controlling enterprise is required to indemnify the AG (Stock Corporation Act, s 311). If the indemnification has not taken place by the end of the fiscal year of the controlled AG, the controlling enterprise is liable for damages suffered thereby by the controlled AG and by fellow shareholders (s 317). In case a shareholder intentionally uses his influence to induce board members or certain key employees to act to the company's detriment, the AG, and possibly other shareholders, may claim damages (s 117). Finally, the exercise of continuous and intensive influence by any party over an AG is considered in legal literature to be incompatible with the independent position of the management board and, therefore, also entails the risk of damage claims.

The above-mentioned rules protecting an AG from undue influence by its shareholders in a factual control situation do not apply to a GmbH. By statute, the GmbH enjoys far less protection against its

---

* The following rules applicable to a control agreement also apply to a profit transfer agreement (*Gewinnabführungsvertrag*), i.e. an agreement obligating an AG or GmbH to transfer its entire annual net profit to another enterprise. All such rules applicable to an AG also apply to a KGaA (partnership limited by shares).

shareholders than the AG. In fact, it is a basic principle of the GmbH Act that the supreme authority lies with the shareholders' meeting which can give binding instructions to management with regard to all company matters. However, attempts have been made by legal writers and courts to afford the GmbH a protection approximating that of the AG. Since the mid-1980s, the Federal Supreme Court has developed in several landmark decisions a new concept of shareholder liability applicable to enterprises controlling a GmbH without a control agreement. At this time, the "TBB"-decision of March 1993 marks the latest word of the Federal Supreme Court on shareholder liability based on control (Federal Supreme Court, decision of 29th March 1993, ZIP 1993, 589 (*"TBB"*)). According to this decision, which clarifies and restricts previous case law, a controlling shareholder may become personally liable if he intentionally or negligently abuses his position by not taking adequate consideration of the interests of the GmbH.

The exercise of control *per se*, even if continuous and intensive, does not result in liability. It is the abuse of control that makes the shareholder liable. This new concept of shareholder liability applies only if the GmbH suffers losses which cannot be attributed to specific acts of the controlling shareholder, e.g. because of their number and complexity or due to insufficient bookkeeping, so that the controlling shareholder cannot be held responsible for specific acts under different concepts of liability.

(3) *Rights of Creditors*

As a rule, only the corporation or other shareholders are entitled to indemnification or damages both under control agreements and in factual control situations. Creditors have normally no direct claim against the controlling shareholder, but they may seize the company's claim in enforcement of a judgment which they have obtained against the company in court. If the corporation goes bankrupt and no bankruptcy proceedings are opened due to the lack of funds, the creditors may, in certain cases, also be entitled to bring their claims directly against the controlling enterprise. In addition, the Stock Corporation Act provides that upon termination of a control agreement the controlling enterprise has to provide security for its creditors (Stock Corporation Act, s 303).

4. Sources of Information

(a) Commercial Registry

The primary source of information about a potential target is the commercial registry.

Almost all commercial enterprises must be registered in the commercial register (*Handelsregister*) kept by the commercial registry, which is a department of the local courts. Registration of an enterprise has to take place with the commercial registry of the local courts competent for its domicile.

The commercial register is designed to provide essential and current legal information on the enterprises registered therein. It indicates, *inter alia*, the firm names, addresses and purposes of business, the owners of sole proprietorships, the partners of partnerships, the share capital of corporations, the persons having authority of representation, the composition of supervisory boards and the opening of bankruptcy proceedings. The articles of corporations are also on file with the commercial registry. However, the shareholders of a GmbH or AG will not be registered in the commercial register. The GmbH has only to file, once every year, with the commercial registry a list of its shareholders, stating the amount of shares held by each shareholder and the identity of each shareholder (GmbH Act, s 40, para 1). It also has to notify the commercial registry when all the shares of the company have come under the control of a single shareholder (GmbH Act, s 40 para 2). An AG which is controlled by one single shareholder has the same obligation (Stock Corporation Act, s 42). Moreover, corporations have to file their financial statements, as specified in further detail on pp. 35–37 below.

The commercial register as well as the files relating thereto (*Registerakten*) are open to inspection by the public and copies of the register and the files may be requested. The access of foreigners to the register and to the files is in no way limited. Indeed, registrations in the commercial register must in any event be published by the court in the Federal Gazette (*Bundesanzeiger*) and in at least one other newspaper.

(b) Further Sources

Another source of information is provided by the so-called corporate gazettes (*Gesellschaftsblätter*), in which AGs are required to publish certain information about themselves. For instance, notices of shareholders' meetings, including the agenda, and the financial statements of large AGs must be published in this way. The corporate gazettes of an AG are designated in its articles of association and must include, and may be limited to, the Federal Gazette (*Bundesanzeiger*).

In addition, businesses are subject to various disclosure obligations which will be discussed on p. 30 *et seq.* below. Disclosures made in this connection may contain meaningful information for an investor.

There are, of course, special information rights for shareholders and partners respectively. Examples of such information rights are given on p. 20 above in connection with the topic of minority protection.

Finally, information may be obtained through credit agencies or discreet banking channels. Bank information plays an important role in Germany and should not be overlooked by a purchaser. However, given that German banks are substantial shareholders in many listed AGs, this may compromise the purchaser's desire for confidentiality.

III. THE REGULATORY FRAMEWORK

1. General

German merger and acquisition practice is quite different from that in many other countries, particularly the US and Great Britain. Acquisitions in Germany are traditionally made by private agreement. Large-scale takeover battles of the kind witnessed in the US and Great Britain have no equivalent in the German market. Tender offers are of relatively little importance and proxy solicitations and proxy fights are unheard of.

Apart from the merger control provisions of the Antitrust Act (*Gesetz gegen Wettbewerbsbeschränkungen*), there are few rules of German law dealing specifically with acquisitions. It has been a widely accepted position in the German business community that the introduction of statutory provisions is unnecessary since competition is sufficiently protected by the Antitrust Act and any other interests are adequately taken care of by voluntary compliance with non-binding guidelines. This situation is changing, though. The harmonisation efforts of the EU Commission and the growing consensus among market participants that the regulatory environment in Germany was not quite up to international standards have produced a more detailed regulatory framework by the adoption of the Second Act on the Promotion of Financial Markets (*Zweites Finanzmarktförderungsgesetz*) of July 1994. This Act has brought about a new Securities Trading Act (*Wertpapier-handelsgesetz*) and major changes of existing laws, such as the Stock Exchange Act (*Börsengesetz*) and the Stock Corporation Act. It provides for a package of measures, in particular anti-insider dealing legislation, disclosure rules and the establishment of a new Federal Securities Supervisory Authority (*Bundesaufsichtsamt für den Wertpapierhandel*), which are designed to enhance the international competitive position of Germany as a financial centre.

2. Restrictions on Acquisitions by Non-Residents; Exchange Control

Germany has a very liberal attitude towards investment by foreigners. There are almost no restrictions affecting acquisitions by non-residents and the movement of capital is entirely free.

(a) Exchange Control

Under the Foreign Trade Act (*Aussenwirtschaftsgesetz*) the Government has the right to restrict foreign trade and exchange in order to counteract any adverse effects on the purchasing power of the German mark or to ensure the stability of the balance of payments. On this basis, the Government may restrict, *inter alia*, the acquisition of domestic companies, real estate, ships and securities by non-residents as well as the importation and exportation of capital (Foreign Trade Act, ss 22 and 23). No such restrictions are in force at present, nor are they anticipated in the foreseeable future.

The acquisition of an interest in a German business is not subject to any exchange or foreign trade control. Furthermore, there are no limitations on the transfer of profits, dividends, interest or royalties by non-residents, except for applicable withholding or capital gains taxes and, once invested, capital may be freely re-transferred.

(b) Reporting Requirements

The Foreign Trade Regulation (*Aussenwirtschaftsverordnung*) requires that certain cross-border transactions be reported to the Federal Bank (*Bundesbank*) through the competent State Central Bank (*Landeszentralbank*). The reporting requirement applies, for instance, to capital investments exceeding DM100,000, including participations in enterprises of more than 20%, as well as to payments exceeding DM5000 (Foreign Trade Regulation, ss 57, 58a and 59). It merely serves statistical purposes and does not in any way restrict foreign investors.

(c) Selected Business-Oriented Restrictions

Only in a very few sensitive areas is there any specific control of foreign investment. For example, under the Aviation Act (*Luftverkehrsgesetz*) an aircraft may in general be registered in the German Aircraft Register only if it is owned by German nationals or by a company domiciled in Germany and under the control (in terms of shareholding and management) of German nationals. The War Armaments Control Act (*Kriegswaffenkontrollgesetz*) provides that the licence necessary to produce or distribute armaments may be denied if the granting of such licence would interfere with the interests of the German Government in maintaining friendly relations with other countries or if a member of the management of the company applying for the licence is not a German national. Finally, some States of the Federal Republic have enacted legislation under which the acquisition of real estate by non-EU foreigners requires governmental approval.*

3. General Restrictions on Acquisitions

(a) Licensing Requirements

In some fields of business, such as banking, insurance, pharmaceuticals, nuclear energy, public transportation and gastronomy, a public licence is required for the operation of a business. The licence may be denied if the management of the company applying for the licence is insufficiently qualified or reliable. These licensing requirements apply regardless of whether the owners of the company are residents or nonresidents and do not discriminate against foreign investors.

A licence held by a company will not normally be affected by a change of ownership in such company, provided that the management of the company remains the same. On the other hand, if only the assets of a licensed business are being acquired, it may be that those assets include some types of licences which cannot be transferred and therefore have to be applied for anew by the acquiror.

Somewhat an exception to the rule that only the operation of a certain business may require a licence, but not the acquisition of an interest in the company operating such business, may be found in the banking area. As from 1st January 1993, any proposed acquisition of an "essential interest" (as a rule, 10% or more of the capital or voting rights) in a German bank has to be notified to the Banking Supervisory Authority (*Bundesaufsichtsamt für das Kreditwesen*) and to the Bundesbank (Banking Act, ss 2b and 1, para 9). The same is true for increases of essential interests beyond certain thresholds. The Banking Supervisory Authority may prohibit the proposed acquisition or increase of an interest if it finds that the acquirer is not sufficiently reliable or that, because of a particularly close relationship between the acquirer and the bank, no effective supervision of the bank is possible. This new control mechanism has been introduced in connection with broader

---

* Such restrictions have been imposed on the basis of articles 86 and 88 of the Introductory Act to the Civil Code (*EGBGB*) and are applicable in Schleswig-Holstein, Berlin and the Saarland.

measures to fight money laundering and influence by organised crime on financial institutions.

(b) Restrictions under Company Law

German company law does not impose any restrictions on the acquisition of interests in domestic companies by foreigners. However, the articles of association or partnership agreement, as the case may be, may restrict the transfer of interests in such companies. It may be provided, for instance, that a transfer (to a foreigner) is not valid unless approved by the management, supervisory board or shareholders and partners, respectively. In the case of an AG, such a restriction would be valid only with regard to registered shares (*Namensaktien*) issued by the company. Even where the transfer of interests is unrestricted, the articles or the partnership agreement may limit the voting rights attaching to the interests held by any single party or entity to a certain ceiling (e.g. 5% of the aggregate capital). Restrictions on the acquisition of interests and on the exercise of voting rights are defensive tactics which can be applied regardless of the nationality of the prospective acquiror. Some major AGs have in fact used these methods to ward off large-scale foreign investments and to protect themselves against hostile takeovers.

(c) Merger Control

General restrictions on acquisitions are imposed by the merger control rules of the Act against Restraints of Competition. These rules are dealt with on p. 46 *et seq.* below. The rules of EU merger control are dealt with on p. 52 *et seq.* below.

4. Disclosure Obligations

There is no general requirement for "capital market disclosure" as is the case, for example, in the US. Specific disclosure obligations may be found in various statutes, some of these being limited to specific company forms.

(a) Disclosure Relating to Marketing of Securities

The admission of securities to trading in the official or regulated market on a German stock exchange is granted only on the basis of a prospectus. Moreover, as from 1st January 1991 a prospectus must be published, as a matter of principle, for all securities which are offered to the public for the first time in Germany and which are not admitted to trading on a German stock exchange. The contents of the prospectus varies depending on the applicable statutes.* Generally speaking, the prospectus must contain all information which is necessary to enable the public to make a proper assessment of the issuer and the securities being offered.

(b) Disclosure Relating to Listed Securities (Periodic and ad hoc Disclosure)

Once securities have been listed on a German stock exchange, the issuer has on-going broad disclosure obligations. The applicable rules are quite detailed and vary depending on the type of securities involved and the type of listing attained.

The basic rule is that the issuer of securities admitted to the official market has to inform the public and the admission office (*Zulassungsstelle*) adequately about the issuer and the admitted securities (Stock Exchange Act, s 44, para 1, No. 3). Specific obligations following from such rule comprise in particular the following:

- the issuer of shares has to publish any notice of shareholders' meetings and informations on the payment of dividends, the issuance of new shares and the exercise of exchange and subscription rights (Stock Exchange Admission Regulation, s 63, para 1);
- the issuer of shares has to inform the admission office about proposed amendments of its articles of association (Stock Exchange Admission Regulation, s 64, para 1);
- the issuer of securities has to make available its financial statements to the public through the paying agent (*Zahlstelle*), unless the statements are published in Germany (s 65, para 1).

Furthermore, the issuer of shares admitted to the official market is required to publish regularly at least one interim report during each fiscal year giving a true and fair view of the financial situation and the general condition of the issuer's business during the period under review (Stock Exchange Act, s 44b, para 1 and Stock Exchange Admission Regulation, s 53 *et seq*).

The periodic disclosure afforded by the regular publication of financial statements and interim reports is supplemented by a requirement of ad hoc disclosure in certain cases. The issuer of securities admitted to

---

* Listings are dealt with in the Stock Exchange Act (*Börsengesetz*) and the Stock Exchange Admission Regulation (*Börsenzulassungsverordnung*). Public offerings are covered by the Securities Prospectus Act (*Wertpapier-Verkaufsprospektgesetz*) and the Offering Prospectus Regulation (*Verkaufsprospekt-Vorordnung*).

the official or regulated market of a German stock exchange has to disclose without delay all new facts unknown to the public which have occurred within its field of activity and which, because of their influence on the assets, the financial situation or the business of the issuer, might have a significant effect on the price of its admitted securities or which, in the case of bonds, might impair the issuer's ability to meet its obligations. The Securities Supervisory Authority can exempt the issuer upon application from its obligation to disclose if the disclosure might be harmful to the legitimate interests of the issuer (Securities Trading Act, s 15). Non-compliance with the obligation of ad hoc disclosure is punishable as an administrative offence by fines of up to DM3m (Securities Trading Act, s 39).

The obligation of ad hoc disclosure poses a number of difficult questions. The *Guide on Insider Dealing and Ad Hoc Disclosure under the Securities Trading Act,** provides a first non-authoritative interpretation of the law which can be seen as an attempt by German industrial and financial institutions to set uniform standards. The *Guide* gives numerous examples of facts which might have a significant effect on the price of securities (such as the sale of core businesses, mergers, reorganisations, control agreements, profit transfer agreements, acquisition or sale of major interests, takeover bids, capital increases or decreases, commencement or discontinuation of core activities, important agreements with third parties, important inventions). Whether an obligation to disclose actually exists, however, has to be established on the basis of all relevant circumstances. Not every inside information (insider fact) which is subject to the prohibition of insider dealing must necessarily be disclosed. This is typically the case for corporate decision processes which develop in multiple steps. If, for instance, a decision of the management board to acquire another company requires the consent of the supervisory board, normally the decision of the management board will be an insider fact, but no ad hoc disclosure of such decision will be necessary before the supervisory board has given its consent.

(c) **Disclosure Relating to Major Holdings of Shares**

The Stock Corporation Act provides for general disclosure obligations when shares in an AG or a KGaA are acquired.

As soon as an enterprise — be it German or foreign — owns more than 25% of the shares of an AG or a KGaA, it has to report such

---

* *Insiderhandelsverbote und ad hoc-Publizität nach dem Wertpapierhandelsgesetz,* published 1994 by Deutsche Börse AG in cooperation with the German stock exchanges and the top associations of German industry and finance.

participation to the company in writing without delay. The acquisition of a majority interest again triggers the reporting obligation. It does not make any difference whether the shares are held directly, through a subsidiary or through a third party acting for the account of the acquiring entity. Even shares subject only to a call option, or which may have to be acquired under a put option, will count for reporting purposes. Any discontinuation of these levels of shareholding must also be reported to the AG and the KGaA respectively.

The report merely has to indicate that more than 25% of the shares or a majority interest has been acquired. It is not necessary to disclose the precise percentage acquired, except in cases of mutual participations in excess of 25%.

The AG or KGaA which has received such a report can at any time request that it be given evidence of the existence of the participation. Upon receipt of the report, the company must publish the existence of the participation and the name of its holder in the company gazettes. It must also disclose such participation in the annex of notes (*Anhang*) to its financial statements.

For so long as a report required under the Stock Corporation Act has not been made, the rights relating to the relevant participation cannot be exercised. In particular, no voting rights may be exercised and no dividends may be received on such shares.

Where an AG or KGaA acquires shares in another German corporation, the above disclosure obligations are also applicable to a substantial degree.

The afore-mentioned general disclosure obligations under the Stock Corporation Act have been supplemented and considerably expanded by the new Securities Trading Act (*Wertpapierhandelsgesetz*) of July 1994. In implementation of the EC Transparency Directive of December 1988, German law now requires that any person that acquires or disposes of an interest in a listed corporation and, following such acquisition or disposal, reaches, exceeds or falls below one of the thresholds of 5%, 10%, 25%, 50% or 75% of the voting rights, shall notify thereof both the corporation and the new Securities Supervisory Authority (Securities Trading Act, s 21, para 1). The notice shall be given in writing without delay, at the latest within seven calendar days, and shall also set forth the exact percentage of the interest held and the address of the person giving the notice. "Listed corporation" shall mean any corporation which has its domicile in Germany and the shares of which have been admitted to the official market of a stock exchange within the EU or an EEA member state (s 21, para 2). A listed corporation which has received any such notice shall disclose the information so obtained. A foreign corporation admitted to the official market of a German stock exchange is subject to a comparable disclosure obligation as soon as it learns that one of its shareholders reaches, exceeds or falls below one of the afore-mentioned thresholds (s 26).

In order to make the new disclosure obligations effective and to avoid circumventions, the voting rights which are considered to be held by a party for disclosure purposes have been defined in a broad fashion. Voting rights attributable to the following shares are deemed equivalent to the voting rights of the party required to notify and, therefore, are attributed to such party (s 22):

- shares owned by a third party which are held for the account of the party required to notify or for the account of an enterprise controlled by the party required to notify;
- shares owned by an enterprise controlled by the party required to notify;
- shares owned by a third party with whom the party required to notify or an enterprise controlled by it has entered into an agreement obliging both parties to the agreement to pursue long-term joint purposes regarding the management of the company by exercising their voting rights in concert;
- shares assigned by the party required to notify to a third party as collateral, unless such third party is authorised to exercise the voting rights attributable to such shares and expresses its intention to do so;
- shares in which the party required to notify has been granted a right of usufruct (*Nießbrauch*);
- shares which can be acquired by the party required to notify or an enterprise controlled by it by the exercise of a call option;
- shares placed in custody with the party required to notify, provided that such party may exercise the voting rights attributable to such shares in its own discretion if no special instructions by the shareholder are given.

For so long as the notice required of the shareholder has not been given, the voting rights relating to the relevant shares held by such shareholder or enterprises controlled by it may not be exercised (s 28). Furthermore, non-compliance with the notice requirement is subject to administrative fines of up to DM500,000 (s 39).

The expanded disclosure obligations will result in improved transparency in the German securities market. At the same time, it will no longer be possible to accumulate secretly substantial interests in a company as a springboard for a tender offer (so-called "creeping-in").

(d) Notification of Share Transfers

When shares in a GmbH or registered shares in an AG are transferred, the company has to be notified of the transaction. Such notification is not a requirement for the validity of the transfer. However, the company must continue to treat the transferor as the shareholder (particularly for voting and dividend purposes) and cannot recognise the transferee as the new owner until the notification has been made. For this reason, a purchaser of shares should notify the target company of his acquisition, once completed, as soon as possible.

(e) Disclosure to Commercial Registry

There are also substantial disclosure obligations vis-à-vis the commercial registry (see pp. 25–26). Non-compliance with such disclosure obligations may result in different legal consequences. Whereas in some cases the transaction to be disclosed does not become effective until its disclosure, in other cases the relevant transaction *does* become effective, even without disclosure, but the commercial registry can impose administrative fines for non-disclosure. In other instances, non-disclosure has no consequences at all.

(f) Financial Disclosure

The Commercial Code (*Handelsgesetzbuch*) requires, as a rule, all corporations to make their financial statements publicly available. The extent to which this has to be done depends on the classification of the corporation as large, medium-sized or small, this classification being uniform in all EU countries.

Large corporations have to publish their financial statements (balance sheet, profit and loss statement and annex of notes) together with the auditor's certificate or statement of refusal, the business report (*Lagebericht*), the report of the supervisory board and certain other financial information in the Federal Gazette (*Bundesanzeiger*) and file this information with the competent commercial registry where they are subject to inspection by the public (Commercial Code, s 325, para 2). Large corporations are those which exceed at least two out of the following three criteria in two consecutive business years (s 267, para 3):

- DM15,500,000 balance sheet total;
- DM32,000,000 sales;

- 250 employees as annual average.

In addition, a corporation is always deemed to be large if its shares or other securities issued by it are admitted to the official or regulated market or traded in the semi-official market of a stock exchange in an EU country, or if admission to the official or regulated market has been applied for.

Medium-sized corporations have to file with the commercial registry the same documents as large corporations, except that they enjoy some relief with regard to the required contents of the balance sheet and the annex of notes (Commercial Code, s 327). They are not obliged to publish these documents in the Federal Gazette but they have to publish a notice in the Federal Gazette indicating with which commercial registry and under which number such documents have been filed (s 325, para 1). Medium-sized corporations are those which qualify neither as large nor as small corporations (s 267, para 2).

Small corporations are subject to rather limited financial disclosure requirements. They have to file with the commercial registry basically only their balance sheet and annex of notes but not their profit and loss statement (Commercial Code, s 326, para 1). No publication of these documents in the Federal Gazette is required. However, small corporations have to publish in the Federal Gazette a notice indicating with which commercial registry and under which number the filing was made (s 325, para 1). Small corporations are those which do not exceed at least two of the following three criteria in two consecutive business years (s 267, para 1):

- DM3,900,000 balance sheet total;
- DM8,000,000 sales;
- 50 employees as annual average.

A German parent corporation of a group of companies (*Konzern*) is in general required to prepare and disclose consolidated financial statements and a consolidated business report on a worldwide basis covering all of its subsidiaries (Commercial Code, ss 290 *et seq.*, 325 *et seq.*).

Large enterprises which have not been organised in the form of a corporation, in particular commercial partnerships and sole proprietorships, are subject to the financial disclosure requirements under the Disclosure Act (*Publizitätsgesetz*). In order to qualify under the Disclosure Act, at least two of the three following criteria have to be exceeded (Disclosure Act, s 1):

- DM125,000,000 balance sheet total;

- DM250,000,000 sales;
- 5,000 employees.

Enterprises which qualify under the Disclosure Act have basically the same disclosure obligations as large corporations under the Commercial Code.

It may be added that, except for larger companies, the German business community so far has been quite reluctant to comply with the financial disclosure requirements. The authority of the competent commercial registry to enforce the disclosure obligation by assessing administrative fines of up to DM10,000 is of a somewhat theoretical nature because the registry may act only upon the request of a shareholder, a creditor or the works council (*Betriebsrat*) of the delinquent company. The EU Commission has requested that Germany introduce more effective sanctions against non-compliance but the Federal Government refused to do this because it held the view that the protection of small and medium-sized businesses should take priority over the disclosure requirement. Since the dispute could not be settled, the EU Commission has initiated legal proceedings in the European Court of Justice claiming that Germany has not fulfilled its obligations under the EC Treaty and the First and Fourth Directive.*

(g) Disclosure in Tender Offers

The Takeover Code provides for various disclosure obligations in the context of a tender offer. This will be discussed in the following section.

5. Takeover Code

For the reasons set out on pp. 76–80 below, tender offers have not been frequently used in takeover activities in Germany. This may explain why there have hitherto been no statutes specifically governing tender offers. The conduct of parties involved in voluntary public tender offers has so far only been subject to recommendations by the Stock Exchange Expert Commission (*Börsensachverständigenkommission*) created by the Ministry of Finance.

In 1979 the Stock Exchange Expert Commission issued Guidelines on Voluntary Public Tender Offers (*Leitsätze für öffentliche freiwillige Kauf- und Umtauschangebote*). The Guidelines were considered as insufficient and lagging considerably behind the standard of other European jurisdictions, in particular of England and France. In July 1995 the Stock

---

* Complaint filed on 16th June 1995 (Legal Matter C-191/95).

Exchange Expert Commission issued revised Guidelines under the name "Takeover Code" (*Übernahmekodex*) which came into effect on 1st October 1995.

The express purpose of the new Code is to ensure that public tender offers address all aspects required for an informed decision by both the holders of securities and the target company. The Code is designed to prevent market manipulations and to ensure that all parties act in good faith. The Takeover Code is characterised by the following main new features:

* The offeror who has exceeded the threshold of 50% of the voting rights of the target company, thus becoming a majority shareholder, is in general obliged to make within 21 months an offer for the purchase of the remaining shares ("compulsory offer").

* The price of the compulsory offer shall be not more than 25% below the price which the majority shareholder has paid for shares of the target company within the last six months prior to exceeding the 50% threshold.

* A Takeover Commission (*Übernahmekommission*) with an Executive Office (*Geschäftsstelle*) is created which shall supervise compliance with the Code and perform arbitration tasks.

The Takeover Code governs voluntary public tender offers to the shareholders of an AG or KGaA (target company) for the acquisition of their shares and other defined securities for a cash consideration or in exchange for other securities. The Code is applicable to any natural or legal person making a public tender offer, regardless of the amount of shares already held or to be acquired by the offerer. Purchases of securities which are neither listed on a German stock exchange nor traded in the semi-official market (*Freiverkehr*), in particular shares in a GmbH or interests in partnerships, are not subject to the Code.

The Takeover Code falls into five basic segments as described below.

(a) Principles

The first six articles cover the principles:

(1) The offeror shall treat all holders of securities of the same class equally (article 1).

(2) The offeror and the target company shall provide all holders of securities affected by the offer with the same information. The information shall be those necessary for the evaluation of the offer

and shall correctly and adequately describe the facts. Once a public offer has been made, the management board of the target company is generally under an obligation to provide other persons who have shown a serious interest in acquiring the target company the same information as provided to the original offeror (article 2).

(3) During the offering period the offeror and the target company shall not do anything which might result in exceptional price movements in the target company's securities or the securities offered in exchange therefor (article 3).

(4) The publication of an offer shall normally be preceded by discussions between the offeror and the target company (article 4).

(5) Before publishing the offer, the offeror must notify the contents of the offer to the target company, the German stock exchanges where the securities of the target company and, if applicable, the securities offered in exchange therefor are listed, the Federal Securities Supervisory Authority and the Executive Office of the Takeover Commission. Thereafter, the offer must be published without delay in at least one national journal for mandatory disclosures (article 5).

(6) The offeror shall retain for the preparation and consummation of the offer an admitted investment firm which has its domicile or a branch in a member state of the European Union (article 6).

(b) Contents of Offer

The Code then sets the elements of the contents of the offer in articles 7–11:

(1) The offer shall include at least the following 18 elements (article 7):

- name of offeror and, if applicable, of investment firm providing services in accordance with article 6;
- name of target company;
- securities for which offer is being made;
- maximum and/or minimum number of securities which the offeror undertakes to acquire and information regarding the allotment procedure under article 10;
- information on purchase price or consideration and on consummation of offer;
- information on the elements which have been essential for the determination of the consideration;
- statement whether the offer may be accepted by declaration of the shareholders of the target company or whether the shareholders are only solicited to offer securities of the target company to the offeror;

- information (as to dates and extent) regarding securities of the target company acquired by the offeror prior to the offer, and on pending agreements on such securities;
- any direct and indirect interests of the target company in the offeror (if known);
- any comments of the target company;
- offering period;
- any conditions to the offer and rights of the offeror to withdraw from the offer;
- information on the intentions pursued by the offeror with regard to the target company and possible effects of a successful offer, in particular on the financial conditions of the offeror and the target company;
- statement that the holders of securities of the target company may withdraw their acceptance of the offer in accordance with article 14;
- the date on which the result of the offer will be disclosed;
- information on the status of any merger control proceedings;
- information on any exemption from the provisions of the Code by the Takeover Commission;
- undertaking of the offeror to comply with the provisions of the Code.

(2) The offer may be subject only to conditions which the offeror cannot make occur (article 9).

(3) In case the offer is accepted for a number of securities exceeding the number which the offeror undertook to acquire (over-subscription), the securities shall be pro rated among the accepting security holders. The allotment procedure shall be explained in the offer (article 10).

(4) The offeror must grant a reasonable period for the evaluation of the decision on the offer. The offering period shall be not less than 28 days and not more than 60 days (article 11).

(c) Obligations of Offeror

The obligations of the offeror are covered in articles 12–17:

(1) The offeror shall report all transactions in securities of the target company effected by the offeror or for its account after the publication of the offer to the Executive Office and make such transactions public within one business day (article 12).

(2) If the offeror acquires securities of the target company during the offering period at terms more favourable than those stated in the

offer, those more favourable terms shall apply to all holders of securities of the same class, even if they have already accepted the offer (article 13).

(3) The offeror may better its offer during the offering period, in particular if a third party has made an offer at more favourable terms during the offering period. In such case the offeror may extend the offering period by a period to be agreed to by the Executive Office. If the offeror so betters its offer, it has to ensure that the holders of securities who have already accepted the original offer are treated equally. Such holders of securities may withdraw their acceptance of the original offer in order to accept the better offer (article 14).

(4) If the offeror submits a better offer within a period which must be stated by the offeror in the original offer and must not be less than 12 months and if within such period no third party has made an offer, the offeror shall grant the respective improvement also to those holders of securities who have accepted the original offer (article 15).

(5) If a person acquires more than 50% of the voting rights of the target company, thus becoming a majority shareholder, it must make an offer within 21 months to purchase also the remaining shares ("compulsory offer"). The price to be offered must bear a reasonable relationship to the prevailing exchange price and shall be not more than 25% below the price which the majority shareholder has paid for shares of the target company within the last six months prior to exceeding the 50% threshold. If the majority shareholder has purchased shares of the target company after exceeding the 50% threshold and before making the compulsory offer at an average price which is higher than the afore-mentioned price, then such higher average price must be offered in the compulsory offer.

The majority shareholder is not obliged to make a compulsory offer for the rest of the shares in four situations where the minority shareholders are deemed sufficiently protected under German law. No compulsory offer is required when within 18 months after exceeding the 50% threshold a resolution is passed (i) to enter into a corporate agreement between the majority shareholder and the target company, (ii) to integrate the target company into the majority shareholder, (iii) to change the legal form of the target company or (iv) to merge the target company into the majority shareholder.

In addition, no obligation to make an offer for the remaining shares exists in the following four cases: (i) the 50% threshold is exceeded with securities which the majority shareholder holds only temporarily for resale purposes; (ii) the majority shareholder has unintentionally acquired more than 50% of the voting rights of the target company and lowers its interest to 50% or less without delay; (iii) within 18 months after exceeding the 50% threshold the shareholders' assembly of the target company has exempted the majority shareholder from its obligation to make a compulsory offer and, prior thereto, the majority shareholder has committed itself to the Executive Office in writing not to exercise its voting rights in respect of this topic; or (iv) the Takeover Commission has exempted the offeror from the obligation to make a compulsory offer (articles 16, 17 and 23).

(d) Obligations of Target Company

The obligations of the target company are covered in articles 18 and 19:

(1) The target company shall publish its reasoned opinion on the offer without delay, at the latest, however, within two weeks after the publication of the offer (article 18).
(2) During the period from the publication of the offer until the publication of its result the boards of the target company and of its affiliates shall not take any actions conflicting with the interest of the holders of securities to accept the offer. The Code gives some examples for actions which, in general, might be so conflicting, namely the issuance of new shares, substantial changes in the assets or liabilities of the target company and the entering into contracts outside the ordinary course of business (article 19).

(e) Takeover Commission

The role of the Takeover Commission is as follows:
(1) The Takeover Commission shall consist of at least seven and at most 15 members who will be appointed by the Stock Exchange Expert Commission for a period of five years. It shall be composed of representatives of issuers, institutional investors, private investors, credit institutions and investment firms (article 20).
(2) Prospective offerors, target companies and investment firms will be requested to acknowledge the Takeover Code as binding. The Executive Office will from time to time publish a list of the companies which have acknowledged the Code. In cases of violations of the Code the Executive Office can publish its observations, recommendations and decisions. Prior to publication, however, the

Executive Office has to hear the parties affected, and they can appeal to the Takeover Commission which will make a final decision (article 21).

(3) The Executive Office shall examine an offer within two weeks after publication for compliance with the Code (article 22).

(4) The Takeover Commission may exempt the offeror or the target company from obligations under the Code if compliance therewith would jeopardise legitimate interests of the offeror, the target company or the shareholders of the target company. This possibility exists also for the obligation to make a compulsory offer (article 23).

(f) Outlook

As stated above, the Takeover Code has no force of law and compliance therewith is voluntary. By the end of 1995, the Code had been acknowledged already by 150 German listed corporations, representing a stock exchange capitalisation of more than 40%. Nevertheless, it appears doubtful whether the Code will gain widespread recognition after the Association of German Industry (*Bundesverband der Deutschen Industrie*) meanwhile has voiced strong reservations against it.

On 10th January 1996, the EU Commission submitted a revision of its proposal for a 13th Company Law Directive on Takeovers, which had been blocked for years. The revised proposal appears to be more flexible and less stringent than the German Takeover Code. In particular, Member States do not have to provide for a compulsory offer in cases where the offeror acquires control if they have introduced other equivalent measures protecting minority shareholders. Whether and to which extent the Takeover Code will survive will largely depend on the final form of the proposed directive and the German statute implementing it.

6. Insider Trading Rules

In implementation of the EC Insider Dealing Directive of 13th November 1989 and in an effort to boost its standing as a financial centre, Germany has passed tough legislation against insider dealing. The Securities Trading Act of July 1994 makes insider dealing a criminal offence and establishes a new Federal Securities Supervisory Authority to police the securities markets. The new law has done away with the former Insider Trading Rules (*Insiderhandels-Richtlinien*) which were only voluntary guidelines and did not constitute an effective protection against the improper use of inside information. The *Guide on Insider Dealing and Ad Hoc Disclosure Under the Securities Trading Act,* published 1994 by Deutsche Börse AG, provides a first non-authoritative interpretation of the statute and gives many illustrative examples (see p. 32 above).

The definition of "insider" is rather broad. It encompasses both the primary insider and the secondary insider. Primary insiders are, essentially, persons who have direct access to inside information either as board members (including general partners) of the issuer or affiliated companies, or as stockholders of the issuer or affiliated companies, or by reason and within the scope of their professional activity or function (e.g. as accountants, lawyers, employees) (Securities Trading Act, s 13, para 1). A secondary insider is any other person who has knowledge of inside information, even if the source of such knowledge is not a primary insider (s 14, para 2).

"Inside information" means any fact which is not publicly known and relates to one or several issuers of insider securities or to insider securities and which, if becoming public, is capable of having a significant effect on the price of the insider securities (s 13, para 1). An analysis made exclusively on the basis of publicly available facts will under no circumstances be considered as inside information (s 13, para 2). The requirement of a "significant effect" is probably the most difficult element to determine. For purposes of practicability it has been suggested to apply fixed percentages (e.g. a change of stock price greater than 5% to be significant). This seems inappropriate, however, because significance is determined by a multitude of factors, including the depth of the market and the type and volatility of the securities concerned. All such factors have to be considered on a case by case basis.

"Insider securities" have been broadly defined as any kind of securities which have been admitted for trading or included in the semi-official market on a German stock exchange or which have been admitted for trading on an officially regulated and supervised market in a member state of the EU or the EEA (ss 12 and 2). In particular, shares, certificates representing shares, bonds, profit participation certificates, warrants and other instruments comparable to shares and bonds as well as certain derivatives qualify as securities.

The law provides that anybody in possession of inside information, whether he is a primary or secondary insider, must not exploit his knowledge of that information by acquiring or selling insider securities of the issuer to which the information relates (s 14, para 1, No. 1 and para 2). It does not make any difference whether the insider acts for his own or a third party's account or on behalf of a third party. In addition, a primary insider is prohibited from tipping a third party both in the form of unauthorised disclosure and making accessible of inside information and in the form of giving recommendations on the basis of inside information to acquire or sell insider securities (s 14, para 1 Nos 2 and 3).

Violations of the insider law qualify as criminal offences which are subject to fines or to imprisonment of up to five years (s 38). Moreover, inside dealing may result in claims for damages against the insider.

The prohibition of insider dealing will be enforced by the new Securities Supervisory Authority. This federal body, initially staffed with some 100 employees, supervises the securities markets in order to prevent and pursue insider dealing. It has far-reaching investigatory powers and cooperates with foreign regulators on the international stage (ss 16 and 19). The criminal prosecution of insider dealing falls within the responsibility of the district attorney's office (s 18).

7. Rules of Conduct

The Securities Trading Act of July 1994 has also brought statutory Rules of Conduct for firms offering investment services (*Verhaltensregeln für Wertpapierdienstleistungsunternehmen*). These Rules of Conduct implement article 10 of the EC Investment Services Directive of May 1993 into German law and replace the former Dealer and Adviser Rules (*Händler- und Beraterregeln*) which did not have the force of law.

The law requires investment firms to comply with a detailed set of general and special rules relating to investor protection, internal organisation and record keeping. The general and special rules relating to investor protection apply in general even to foreign firms insofar as their customers are German (Securities Trading Act, s 31, para 3 and s 32, para 3). Exceptions apply, e.g. for firms providing services exclusively for certain affiliated companies or for transactions on exchanges between investment firms (s 37).

The general rules lay down the basic obligations of investment firms to render investment services with the necessary know-how, care and diligence in the interest of their customers, to avoid conflicts of interests, to obtain information from their customers regarding their experience, goals and finances and to give their customers all relevant information (s 31). The special rules make it illegal for investment firms and affiliated businesses to recommend transactions in securities or derivatives which are not in the customers' interest, to recommend transactions in securities or derivatives in order to manipulate prices for transactions for their own account, or to engage, on the basis of knowledge of a customer's order, in securities or derivatives transactions which might result in disadvantages for the customer (s 32, para 1). Certain key people in investment firms, such as owners, general partners, managing directors, investment advisors and analysts, are subject to the same prohibition (s 32, para 2).

Compliance with the Rules of Conduct is controlled by the new Securities Supervisory Authority, which may also introduce guidelines interpreting such rules (s 35). The Securities Trading Act makes only violations of the rules on record-keeping subject to administrative fines (of up to DM100,000). Violations of other rules may, however, entail sanctions under general laws, such as claims for damages by the customer for breach of contract or even criminal liability for fraud or breach of fiduciary duties.

IV. MERGER CONTROL AND ANTITRUST LAW

1. German Merger Control

(a) General

Merger control by the Federal Cartel Office (*Bundeskartellamt*) pursuant to the Act against Restraints of Competition (*Gesetz gegen Wettbewerbs-beschränkungen*) has a major impact on most acquisitions. Mergers, as defined in the statute, must in general be notified to the Federal Cartel Office in Berlin.

All mergers which have an appreciable effect on the domestic market are subject to merger control regardless of whether domestic or foreign enterprises are involved. This is even true for mergers between foreign enterprises transacted abroad.

(b) Definition of Mergers

The Act against Restraints of Competition contains complex rules defining certain transactions which are considered as "mergers". Transactions not caught by those rules are not subject to merger control and may therefore be neither investigated nor prohibited by the Federal Cartel Office. The following transactions constitute mergers within the meaning of the Act (s 23, para 2):

(1) the *acquisition of* the *assets* of another enterprise in whole or in substantial part by reorganisation or other means;
(2) the *acquisition of shares* in another enterprise (be it by the transfer of existing shares or by subscription for shares in connection with the formation of a new enterprise or in connection with an increase in capital of an existing enterprise) if such shares alone or together with other shares already held by the acquiror equal (i) 25% or (ii) 50% of the capital or voting rights of the other enterprise or (iii) result in the acquiror holding a majority interest in the enterprise. These rules also apply to the acquisition of interests in a partnership. The acquisition of an interest of less than 25% may still constitute a merger if the acquiror is granted by agreement, articles of association, partnership agreement or resolution a legal position equivalent to that of a shareholder in a stock corporation holding more than 25% of the voting capital (who enjoys in particular a so-called blocking minority — *Sperrminorität*) (see p. 15 above) or if the acquisition qualifies as a merger under any of the following definitions (in particular (5) or (6));
(3) certain *corporate agreements* by which an enterprise establishes control over, or receives the profits of, another enterprise;
(4) the establishment of *interlocking directorates* which are deemed to exist if one half or more of the members of the supervisory board (*Aufsichtsrat*), the management board (*Vorstand*) or another management body of two or more enterprises are the same individuals;
(5) any *other affiliation* between enterprises by which one or more enterprises may directly or indirectly exercise a controlling influence over another enterprise;
(6) any affiliation between enterprises of the kind described above under (1), (4) or (5) by which, although the specific requirements set forth therein are not met, one or more enterprises may directly or indirectly exercise a *significant competitive influence* over another enterprise. This rule was introduced in 1990 to catch concentrations which gave an enterprise a significant influence over the competitive behaviour of another enterprise but did not qualify as mergers until then. It has been phrased fairly vaguely and added uncertainty to the definition of mergers.

There are a number of supplementary rules which are intended to expand the applicability of the merger control provisions. The following may be of particular importance in the context of an acquisition:

(7) any merger of enterprises is deemed to constitute a merger of the enterprises controlled by them (Act against Restraints of Competition, s 23, para 3, fourth sentence). This is why a merger of

two foreign companies would also constitute a merger of their German subsidiaries, allowing the Federal Cartel Office to enforce the German merger control rules against such subsidiaries;

(8) the creation of a joint venture company (*Gemeinschaftsunternehmen*) does not merely constitute vertical mergers between each joint venturer and the joint venture company. With respect to the markets in which the joint venture company is or will be active, it is also deemed to constitute a horizontal merger between the joint venturers themselves (s 23, para 2, No. 2, third sentence). A joint venture company has been defined to mean any enterprise in which two or more enterprises hold interests of at least 25% of the capital or voting rights each. In addition to the merger control rules, the creation of a joint venture company is subject to the general rules of antitrust law, in particular the prohibition of horizontal restraints of competition.

(c) Notification

The law differentiates between pre-merger and post-merger notifications to the Federal Cartel Office. A notification of an intended merger may be either mandatory or merely voluntary.

Notice of a planned merger (*Zusammenschlussvorhaben*) *must* be given to the Federal Cartel Office *before* its consummation (*mandatory pre-merger notification*) if

- one of the participating enterprises had sales of DM2bn or more during the last preceeding fiscal year; or
- at least two of the participating enterprises had sales of DM1bn or more each during the last preceeding fiscal year; or
- the merger is to be effected under state law by legislative enactment or some other sovereign act (Act against Restraints of Competition, s 24a, para 1, second sentence).

Notice of a merger plan *may*, as a precautionary measure, be given to the Federal Cartel Office *before* its consummation if the participating enterprises so choose, even though the conditions for mandatory notification are not fulfilled (*voluntary pre-merger notification*) (s 24a, para 1, first sentence).

Every merger must be notified without undue delay *after* its consummation (*post-merger notification*), even if a mandatory or voluntary pre-merger notification was submitted, if the participating enterprises had combined sales of at least DM500m during the fiscal year preceding the merger (s 23, para 1, first sentence, and s 24a, para 3). It follows that, if this threshold is not met, no notification at all is required for merger control purposes.

The sales of an enterprise are computed on a worldwide basis and include the sales of subsidiaries and affiliates. In the case of an acquisition of shares or assets, the seller is not generally considered a participating enterprise so that the seller's sales are not consolidated for these purposes, whereas the sales of the target company or the target business, as the case may be, are consolidated.

Different time limits apply to the investigation and prohibition of the merger and different waiting periods apply to the consummation of a merger depending on whether a pre-merger or post-merger notification is made. Following (voluntary or mandatory) pre-merger notifications and post-merger notifications respectively, periods of up to four months and one year respectively are available to the Federal Cartel Office from receipt of notification to investigate and, if appropriate, to prohibit the merger. The Federal Cartel Office may extend these time limits subject to the consent of the notifying parties. A merger may be prohibited by the Federal Cartel Office only within the statutory time limits. On expiry of the applicable time limit, a merger can no longer be prohibited.

In the case of a mandatory pre-merger notification the law prohibits the parties from either consummating the merger plan or participating in its consummation prior to the expiration of the periods referred to above, unless the Federal Cartel Office notifies them in writing that it does not intend to prohibit the planned merger. Legal transactions in violation of this statutory prohibition are, in general, invalid and may entail administrative fines of up to DM1m. However, it is legally permissible to sign the relevant merger agreement subject to a condition that the merger is notified to and not prohibited by the Federal Cartel Office. In practice, this is usually what happens.

The notification of a merger or planned merger must contain certain information on the form of the merger, the merging enterprises, their sales and domestic market shares but the notification procedure itself is essentially informal.

(d) Prohibition of Mergers

The Federal Cartel Office must prohibit a merger or planned merger if it is expected to result in or strengthen a market-dominating position of one of the parties, unless the parties can demonstrate that the merger also leads to improvements in competition and that such improvements outweigh the disadvantages of market domination (Act

against Restraints of Competition, s 24, paras 1 and 2, first sentence).

There are no detailed statutory standards for determining whether a merger would result in or strengthen a market-dominating position. However, in certain monopoly and oligopoly situations, the law provides that certain market positions, depending on the market shares and number and size of the participants, are presumed to be dominant. This presumption can only be rebutted by showing that the existing market structure indicates that substantial competition can be expected to prevail in the future.

(e) Appeals, Private Suits

A decision of the Federal Cartel Office prohibiting a merger may be appealed to the courts. The courts will then review the factual and legal findings of the Federal Cartel Office.

There is also the possibility of filing a petition for the approval of the merger with the Federal Minister for the Economy. The Minister may grant permission if the restraints of competition effected by the merger are compensated by overall economic advantages of the merger or if the merger is justified by an overriding public interest (Act against Restraints of Competition, s 24, para 3).

The court proceedings and the proceedings before the Minister may be started simultaneously or consecutively. In any event, the decision of the Minister is itself subject to limited review by the courts.

Upon request, the Federal Cartel Office may permit third parties, such as competitors, customers or suppliers of the participants to intervene in merger control proceedings. In no case can third parties sue the participants for injunctive relief or damages or request, as a matter of law, that the Federal Cartel Office investigate or prohibit a merger.

(f) Dissolution

Mergers prohibited by the Federal Cartel Office and not permitted by the Federal Minister for the Economy may be dissolved. This situation may arise where the merger was not subject to pre-merger notification and the parties have chosen first to consummate the transaction and to file a post-merger notification thereafter. However, the Federal Cartel Office is not entitled to prohibit a merger and request its dissolution at the same time. Only after the order of the Federal Cartel Office prohibiting the merger and the refusal of the petition with the Minister (if any) have become final and unappealable may the Federal Cartel Office enforce the dissolution of a merger.

2. Other German Antitrust Law Aspects

The Act against Restraints of Competition distinguishes between various forms of restraint of trade. Apart from mergers, restrictive practices may take the form of cartel agreements, concerted practices, recommendations, boycotts, discriminations and the like. In the context of an acquisition, the parties sometimes enter into agreements which may qualify as cartel agreements and which are for that reason ineffective under the Act.

As a general rule s 1 of the Act against Restraints of Competition declares any agreements between enterprises entered into for a common purpose to be ineffective insofar as they are likely to influence, by restraint of competition, production or market conditions for the sale of goods or commercial services. In addition, concerted practices between enterprises which, if made the subject matter of an agreement, would violate s 1, are prohibited.

This prohibition of cartel agreements (horizontal restraints between actual or potential competitors) covers a broad range of competitive restraints, such as the fixing of prices or of other terms and conditions, the allocation of quotas or territories, the exchange of market data or the establishment of joint selling, purchasing or research organisations, always provided that the agreement is entered into for a common purpose (which is deemed to exist when the restraint is in the mutual interests of the parties). The formation of joint ventures and covenants not to compete require particular attention in merger and acquisition transactions.

The establishment of a joint venture is subject to both merger control and the prohibition of cartel agreements. With regard to the latter, the Federal Cartel Office distinguishes between restraints imposed on the joint venture and restraints imposed on the joint venturers themselves. The joint venturers are free to determine the scope of activities of the joint venture in all respects, e.g. its market, its suppliers and its customers. However, as a rule, the joint venturers are prohibited from expressly or implicitly agreeing on any restraints which might restrict actual or potential competition between themselves or between them-selves and the joint venture. In this respect, joint selling and purchasing organisations are considered likely to restrict competition between the venturers.

Covenants not to compete are often found in acquisition agreements. They usually provide that the seller must not compete for a certain period of time with the business sold. Such agreements, although constituting a restraint of competition, are enforceable provided they are necessary or appropriate to ensure the transfer of the business, including its goodwill, to the buyer. A covenant not to compete for a period of 10 years has been held to be too long but, in practice, periods of between three and five years are commonly agreed upon.

3. EU Merger Control

(a) General

On the EU level, merger control is effected by the EU Commission on the basis of the Council Merger Control Regulation (EEC) No. 4064/89 of 21st December 1989 on the Control of Concentrations between Undertakings (hereinafter the "Merger Control Regulation"). The Merger Control Regulation applies to any transaction which qualifies as a "concentration" and has a "Community dimension".

If a concentration has a Community dimension, it is subject to the exclusive jurisdiction of the EU Commission and, in principle, no Member State shall apply its national competition law (Merger Control Regulation, article 21, para 2). Under special circumstances the Commission may refer a case to the competent authorities of a Member State affected by a concentration which will then apply their national antitrust laws (article 9, para 3(b)). If a concentration has no Community dimension, it falls within the jurisdiction of the Member States which may, however, request that the EU Commission apply the Merger Control Regulation nevertheless, provided that this is necessary to ensure effective competition within the territory of the respective Member States (article 22, para 3).

Due to the high thresholds of the Merger Control Regulation, the number of cases which come to the EU Commission is relatively small. On the basis of the experience gained since 1989, the Commission has made certain proposals for a revision of the Merger Control Regulation, which include a threshold reduction. Those proposals are currently under review by the Member States and a revision of the Merger Control Regulation will possibly take place some time in 1997.

(b) Definition of Concentration

The definition of "concentration" used by the Merger Control Regulation is considerably narrower than the definition of "mergers" applied by the German Act against Restraints of Competition (see pp. 46–48 above). The Merger Control Regulation defines a concentration as:

- the merger of two or more previously independent businesses; or
- the direct or indirect acquisition of control of the whole or parts of one or more businesses by one or more persons already controlling at least one business or by one or more other businesses (article 3, para 1).

Control may be acquired by the purchase of stock or assets, by contract or otherwise. Control is constituted by rights, contracts or any other means which, either separately or in combination and having regard to the factual or legal situation, confer the possibility of exercising decisive influence on a business (article 3, para 3). As a rule, the formation of a cooperative joint venture does not constitute a concentration (but may be subject to Article 85 of the EC Treaty) while the formation of a concentrative joint venture does (article 3, para 2). The Commission has developed certain criteria for how to distinguish concentrative from cooperative joint ventures. The proposed revision of the Merger Control Regulation may bring about new rules for the treatment of joint venture situations.

(c) Definition of Community Dimension

Given the national merger regulations existing in most of the EU Member States, the Merger Control Regulation is designed to cover only cases of concentrations with a Community dimension. A concentration is deemed to have a Community dimension, regardless of where the parties are headquartered or incorporated, if

- the combined aggregate worldwide sales of all of the parties exceed ECU 5bn and
- the aggregate Community-wide sales of each of at least two of the parties exceed ECU 250m,
- unless each of the parties achieves more than two-thirds of its aggregate Community-wide sales within one and the same Member State (article 1, para 2).

(d) Notification and Review Procedure

Concentrations which have a Community dimension must be notified to the EU Commission within one week after the signing of the respective agreement or the announcement of a public bid, whichever occurs first (article 4, para 1). No such concentration must be consummated prior to its notification and the first three weeks following its notification (mandatory pre-merger notification) (article 7, para 1). The Commission may extend or waive the three weeks' waiting period (article 7, paras 2 and 4). A consummation of a transaction prior to the expiration of the applicable waiting period may result in the transaction being ineffective and in the imposition of administrative fines (article 7, para 5, article 14, para 2b).

The notification triggers a two-stage review procedure by the Commission as follows. Within one month following the notification (stage one), the Commission has to make a decision. The decision can be either that the concentration does not fall within the scope of the Merger Control Regulation or that the concentration is not opposed to and declared compatible with the common market or that the concentration raises serious doubts as to its compatibility with the common market and formal proceedings are initiated (article 10, para 1, article 6, para 1b). If the Commission does not take a decision within this time limit, the concentration is deemed declared compatible with the common market (article 10, para 6). In practice, the vast majority of cases is cleared by the Commission within the initial one-month period.

A decision by the Commission to initiate formal proceedings brings the review procedure to stage two where the Commission has to decide at the latest within four more months whether or not the concentration is compatible with the common market (article 10, para 3, article 8, paras 2 and 3). Such decision shall be taken only after the Advisory Committee, consisting of representatives of the Member States, has been heard (article 19, para 3). The parties may modify their original concentration plan during the review process in order to gain clearance by the Commission and the Commission may attach to its decision clearing concentration conditions and obligations to ensure that the parties comply with commitments they have entered into vis-à-vis the Commission (article 8, para 2). If the Commission does not take a decision on the compatibility of the concentration within the four months period for stage two of the review procedure, the concentration is deemed declared compatible with the common market (article 10, para 6).

(e) Standard of Review

The substantive test to be applied by the Commission to a concentration qualifying under the Merger Control Regulation is whether or not the concentration is compatible with the common market (article 2, para 1). A concentration which creates or strengthens a dominant position as a result of which effective competition would be significantly impeded in the common market or in a substantial part of it is incompatible with the common market (article 2, para 3). In making its decision, the Commission shall consider such factors as the competitive situation, the structure of the relevant markets, the market power of the parties and the interests of other participants in the relevant markets (article 2, para 1). In cases where the market power of the enterprises participating in a concentration does not exceed 25% either in the common market or in a substantial part of it, the concentration is, as a rule, considered to be compatible with the common market (recital 15).

(f) EEA Merger Control

With the creation of the European Economic Area (EEA) on 1st January 1994, the competition law of the European Community, including the Merger Control Regulation with its pre-notification requirement and waiting period was extended to Austria, Iceland, Finland, Norway and Sweden*. The EEA is considered a stepping stone to eventual membership in the EU. In fact, Austria, Finland and Sweden have become EU members as from 1st January 1995, making the EU competition laws directly applicable in those countries.

Concentrations which create or strengthen a dominant position as a result of which effective competition would be significantly reduced within the EEA or a substantial part of it are illegal. The EEA has its own competition enforcement agency, the EFTA Surveillance Authority, which reviews concentrations with only an EFTA dimension (turnover of more than ECU 250m by two of the parties in Norway and Iceland). Concentrations that have a Community dimension will continue to fall within the exclusive jurisdiction of the EU Commission, whether or not they also have an EFTA dimension.

V. COMMON TYPES OF TRANSACTION

1. General

Once a target has been identified, the purchaser has to decide upon the method of the acquisition. Depending on the circumstances, the purchaser may have a choice between an asset purchase transaction and a share purchase transaction. Whereas an asset transaction will always be privately negotiated, a share transaction may take various forms. In the vast majority of cases, shares are acquired by private acquisition agreement. However, where the shareholders are numerous and widespread, as is particularly the case with companies listed on a stock exchange, a tender offer may be the only practical method of

---

* Five of the seven states of the European Free Trade Association (EFTA). The remaining EFTA states Switzerland and (so far) Liechtenstein did not join the EEA.

acquisition. A merger may be considered appropriate to effect an amalgamation of companies of comparable size or a reorganisation after the acquisition has taken place. Finally, depending on the purchaser's financing arrangements and the involvement of the target's management with the purchaser, the transaction may take the form of a leveraged or management buy-out.

2. Acquisition of Assets

(a) General

In an asset purchase transaction, the assets and liabilities of the business to be acquired have to be specified and transferred on an individual basis. The specification of the relevant assets and liabilities and the means of their transfer to the purchaser may constitute the most important aspect of an asset purchase transaction. However, there are other aspects to be considered, such as an involuntary assumption of liabilities by operation of law. Furthermore, the tax aspects of the transaction frequently become a dominant issue from the outset and are likely to have important implications for the way the transaction is structured.

(b) Specification of Assets and Liabilities

The assets and liabilities to be acquired have to be defined in the purchase agreement as precisely as possible. The financial statements of the business may serve as a starting point for this purpose. However, important assets and liabilities may not be shown in the balance sheet, such as written-off assets, intellectual property rights, licences, pension liabilities or rights and obligations under agreements. Conversely, assets shown in the balance sheet may in fact be privately owned by a partner of the partnership selling its assets (so-called *Einbringung quoad sortem* or *quoad usum*). Particular care has to be applied in defining the elements constituting the goodwill of the business (e.g. firm name, trade marks, customers, contracts).

The precise identification of the assets to be acquired is not only a vital element of the transaction from a commercial point of view. It is at the same time a requirement of German law. In order to transfer title to tangible assets, it is necessary to describe them in a specified manner in the acquisition agreement or, if there is a separate transfer agreement, in the transfer agreement (so-called "principle of specification"; *Bestimmtheitsgrundsatz*). It must be possible to determine merely from the acquisition agreement (or the transfer agreement, if any), and not by additional reference to other documents, whether or not an individual asset is subject to the transfer. If this is not the case, the transfer of that asset is invalid. Less strict requirements apply to the transfer of rights, claims and liabilities.

The best method of identification and specification is to list the assets and liabilities in schedules to the acquisition agreement. Updated inventory lists, stock lists, accounts receivable lists and the like can be used for this purpose. Since there will generally be a period of time between the signing of the acquisition agreement and the date of completion (during which certain assets listed in the schedules will be disposed of and others will be acquired) the acquisition agreement will also normally classify the assets into specific categories and stipulate that the listed assets will be subject to changes occurring in the ordinary course of business up to the date of completion. Where a longer period between signing and completion is envisaged, it will be necessary to include price adjustments and valuation provisions in the acquisition agreement to take account of this.

(c) Transfer of Assets and Liabilities

German law distinguishes strictly between the contractual obligations to transfer the assets and liabilities and to pay for them on the one hand ("contract of obligation"; *Verpflichtungsgeschäft*) and the actual fulfilment of such obligations on the other hand ("contract of transfer"; *Verfügungsgeschäft*). Both the contractual obligations and their fulfilment may be, and generally are, contained in one single document. Nevertheless, this distinction is of the utmost importance because the transfer of assets and liabilities follows different rules, depending on the individual assets and liabilities concerned.

Moveable assets, such as machinery, equipment, furniture, vehicles, and stocks are transferred by an agreement that title shall pass to the purchaser and by actual delivery (e.g. grant of possession or access). Actual delivery may be replaced by an agreement that the seller shall maintain possession, e.g. as lessee, and the purchaser shall be given indirect possession. Where a third party has possession of the assets to be transferred, actual delivery may be replaced by an assignment to the purchaser of the seller's claim for repossession against such third party.

Real property is transferred by an agreement that title to it shall pass to the purchaser (*Auflassung*) and the registration of the transfer of title in the land register (*Grundbuch*). The obligation to transfer real estate and the *Auflassung* must be contained in a notarised agreement. If real estate is among the assets to be acquired, the entire acquisition agreement must be in notarial form. The form requirement extends to ancillary agreements (including side letters), unless they would have been entered into regardless of the real estate transaction. Failure to notarise the acquisition agreement will result in the invalidity of the entire agreement. A subsequent conveyance in notarial form and registration of the transfer of title in the land register will, however, validate the entire transaction.

Receivables are transferred by a simple assignment agreement. The debtors, generally speaking, need not give their consent to the assignment nor is it necessary to inform them thereof. However, so long as the debtors have no knowledge of the assignment, they may discharge their obligations by paying the seller. Upon notification of the assignment, only a payment to the purchaser will release them from their obligations.

Industrial property rights like trade or service marks (*Marken*), patent rights (*Patente*), utility models (*Gebrauchsmuster*) and protected designs (*Geschmacksmuster*) are transferred by assignment agreement. No particular form is required and the purchaser will be registered in the appropriate register upon application and proof of transfer. Such proof is generally provided by a notarially certified declaration of transfer.

A *firm name* is transferred by assignment agreement. It cannot be transferred without the business to which it relates.

Licences under public law required to operate the business cannot generally be transferred, unless they have been granted for certain installations of the business (so-called *Sachgenehmigungen*). They will have to be applied for anew by the purchaser and the competent authority will examine whether the purchaser has the necessary competence and reliability to be granted his own licence.

Contracts, as a rule, can be transferred by simple assignment agreement only if they expressly provide for this possibility, which is rarely the case. The transfer of a contract normally requires a three-party agreement, i.e. the consent of the other contract party in addition to the assignment agreement. If such consent is given, the contractual position of the seller passes to the purchaser. The acquisition agreement should take precaution against the possibility of refusal by the other contract party to give its consent. The seller and the purchaser may agree to this end to put each other in the position in which they would be, had the contract transfer effectively taken place. This solution will typically include an obligation of the seller to consummate nontransferring contracts for the account of the purchaser and an obligation of the purchaser to indemnify the seller against costs and liabilities resulting from such contracts. Depending on the importance of a contract to be transferred, the consent of the other contract party may even be made a closing condition.

In a few instances, contracts pass to the buyer by operation of law. The most important category of contracts in this respect are employment contracts. If a business or part of a business is transferred, the purchaser assumes the rights and obligations under the employment contracts existing at the date of transfer by operation of law. Further exceptions may be found in relation to leases of real estate and casualty insurance contracts. If real estate leased to a third party is sold to the purchaser, the latter assumes by operation of law all rights and obligations of the lessor under the lease during his term of ownership. Similarily, where assets sold are covered by casualty insurance, all rights and obligations under the insurance contract automatically pass to the purchaser.

The transfer of *liabilities* requires an agreement between seller and purchaser providing for the transfer and, in addition, the consent of the creditor. Alternatively, liabilities can be transferred by agreement between the purchaser and the creditor. Any collateral held by the creditor as security will be extinguished by the transfer. A secured creditor will therefore normally make his consent dependent on the provision of new security by the purchaser. As long as the creditor withholds his consent to a transfer agreed upon between seller and purchaser, the purchaser is under an obligation towards the seller to satisfy the creditor. In other words, although the seller remains primarily liable to the creditor, the purchaser has, as a private contractual matter, to fulfil the obligations of the seller and to indemnify him against claims of the creditor.

An important restriction applies to the transfer of *pension liabilities*. Pension liabilities towards former employees having vested pension rights and towards pensioners can be transferred, even with the consent of the former employee, only to a new employer, a pension fund (*Pensionskasse*), a life insurance company or a pension fund incorporated under public law. Therefore, the purchaser can effectively only assume the pension liabilities of those employees whose contracts of employment are actually being transferred to the purchaser. With regard to pension liabilities to former employees and pensioners who are not being transferred, an assumption of pension liabilities by the purchaser would have no external effect although it would commit the purchaser in its internal relationship with the seller.

(d) Statutory Assumption of Liabilities

A purchaser should be aware that there are three general concepts under which liabilities of the seller can pass to the purchaser by operation of law. These concepts may result in an involuntary assumption of liabilities which the purchaser had intended to exclude from the acquisition and which have not been reflected in the purchase price.

First, a purchaser acquiring all or substantially all of the seller's assets becomes liable for the seller's obligations existing at that point in time under s 419 of the Civil Code (*Bürgerliches Gesetzbuch*). Even the acquisition of a single asset may trigger this liability if the purchaser knows that such asset constitutes all or substantially all of the seller's assets. In order to avoid liability under this section, the seller should retain about 20% of his unencumbered assets. The purchase price obtained by the seller does not qualify as assets for the purposes of s 419 of the Civil Code.

The liability of the purchaser under s 419 is limited to the assets acquired and his claims against the seller under the acquisition agreement. The seller remains jointly and severally liable together with the purchaser. As between themselves, either the purchaser or the seller will have an obligation to hold the other harmless, depending on which party has to bear the relevant liabilities under the acquisition agreement. Section 419 of the Civil Code will be abolished as from 1st January 1999.

Second, if the purchaser acquires a business and continues such business under its previous firm name, s 25 of the Commercial Code (*Handelsgesetzbuch*) provides that he assumes by operation of law all liabilities of the seller which have been created in the conduct of the business. The purchaser can agree with the seller that this assumption of liabilities be excluded. However, such an exclusion will be binding on creditors only insofar as they have been notified thereof or if it has been registered in the commercial register and officially made public. The liability of the purchaser, if not effectively excluded, is unlimited. There is no limitation confining liability to the assets of the business acquired. The seller's liability remains unaffected, though it will in general become statute-barred after five years at the latest.

Third, under s 75 of the Tax Code (*Abgabenordnung*), the purchaser of an entire business or of a discrete business division becomes, by operation of law, liable for all business taxes (e.g. trade tax and value added tax) and withholding taxes (e.g. wage tax) accrued therein as from the beginning of the last calendar year prior to the acquisition. The purchaser's liability is limited to the assets acquired. It cannot be excluded by agreement with the seller and the seller's liability to pay the taxes up to the date of completion remains unaffected.

Besides the afore-mentioned general concepts of law, a buyer may involuntarily assume liabilities where contracts transfer by operation of law or where liabilities attach to specific assets acquired. For instance:

- If a business or part of a business is transferred, the purchaser automatically assumes the rights and obligations under existing employment contracts (see pp. 131–134).
- The acquisition of real estate can render the buyer responsible for existing contamination and clean-up costs.
- The distribution of defective products acquired may subject the buyer to product liability.
- The purchaser of a share in a GmbH is liable for all outstanding capital contributions of both the seller and any other shareholders (see p. 22 above).
- The purchaser of an interest of a limited partner in a limited partnership can become personally liable to the extent the fixed capital contribution of the seller has not been paid up or has been repaid. If the interest is effectively transferred to the purchaser before the purchaser has been registered in the commercial register as the new limited partner, the purchaser will even be subject to unlimited liability for any debt of the partnership incurred between the transfer of the interest and its registration in the commercial register (Commercial Code, s 176, para 2).

As a rule, a statutory transfer of liabilities cannot be contracted out in the acquisition agreement. Nevertheless, the parties will regularly provide for representations and indemnifications by the seller. A cautious purchaser may in addition look for security in the form of a bank guarantee or a hold back from the purchase price.

(e) Bona Fide Acquisition

Tangible assets may be acquired by a purchaser acting in good faith, even though the seller has no title to them. This is true for both moveable assets and real property.

As a rule, a buyer can acquire title to moveable assets even if they are owned by somebody other than the seller, provided that the buyer acts in good faith at the time of acquisition. The buyer is deemed not to be in good faith if he is aware or, due to gross negligence, unaware that the seller lacks ownership and the right to dispose of the asset.

With regard to real estate, the purchaser is even better protected. He may rely on the registration of the seller in the land register and will acquire title unless he positively knows that the seller is not the owner or a protest against the correctness of the land register (*Widerspruch*) has been registered. The foregoing rules apply *mutatis mutandis* to the acquisition of encumbered tangible assets. This means that a purchaser in good faith can acquire assets free of existing encumbrances.

There is, in general, no possibility of a *bona fide* acquisition of moveable assets which have been lost or stolen. Furthermore, intangible assets, such as receivables, industrial property rights and interests in or shares of companies may not be acquired in good faith, unless they are evidenced by negotiable instruments.

The possibility of acquiring tangible assets by reason of the purchaser's *bona fides* is certainly an advantage of an asset purchase transaction, an advantage which a share deal generally does not confer. Nonetheless, this is hardly ever a determining consideration when the method of acquisition is chosen.

(f) Tax Aspects

The tax aspects of asset transactions will be dealt with on pp. 119–121 below.

3. Acquisition of Shares

(a) General

When shares or interests in a company are acquired, there is no need for a conveyance of individual assets and liabilities. Title to the assets and liabilities constituting the business is unaffected by the acquisition and the assets and liabilities remain within the company. Only the shares or interests in the company need to be transferred. This holds true for an acquisition of both shares in a corporation and interests in a commercial partnership. For the purpose of pp. 62–70 the term "shares" includes interests in a commercial partnership.

Where the purchaser does not acquire all the shares of the target company, he will have to evaluate the legal implications connected with his level of shareholding. If he wants to exercise control or undertake structural changes (e.g. an increase or reduction of capital or a reorganisation or merger), he must consider what percentage of the voting capital he needs in order to achieve this. Conversely, if he only wants a small shareholding, it will be important to know what rights a minority shareholder will have. The answers to these questions depend on the nature of the company as well as on the provisions of its articles of association or partnership agreement, as the case may be (see p. 18 *et seq.*).

(b) Scope of Transfer

It is often said that one of the attractions of a share purchase transaction lies in its simplicity. This may be somewhat misleading because the parties to a share transaction also have to define precisely the extent to which rights and obligations are to be transferred.

Most importantly, agreement has to be reached with regard to dividends or profits for the current business year. Unless the parties agree otherwise, the seller of shares is entitled to dividends and profits respectively for the current business year on a pro rata basis until the completion date, i.e. the date of transfer of the shares (Civil Code, s 101, No 2). This statutory consequence can be risky for the seller since he will not be able to influence the results of the remainder of the business year after the buyer has assumed control. Therefore, the seller may want to obtain his share of the profit for the current business year in the form of an increased purchase price (which can also be advantageous from a tax point of view when shares in a corporation are being sold). Sometimes the parties provide that the seller shall be entitled to the profit accruing up to the completion date, which will invariably require the preparation of an interim profit and loss statement.

In the case of transfer of a share in a corporation, claims of the seller against the corporation, in particular claims for the repayment of loans to the corporation, will not transfer to the purchaser, unless otherwise agreed upon.

When an interest in a partnership is transferred, it is generally understood that the capital account (*Kapitalkonto*) of the seller reflecting his equity interest will pass to the purchaser. There are usually additional partnership accounts, such as the reserve account (*Rücklagenkonto*), the private account (*Privatkonto, Kapitalkonto II* or *Darlehenskonto*) and the loss carry-forward account (*Verlustvortragskonto*). In order to avoid disputes, it is highly advisable to specify in the acquisition agreement precisely which accounts of the seller are to be included in the transfer and to arrange for the seller to guarantee the balances on the respective accounts as at the completion date.

In the case of an acquisition of shares in a GmbH which have not been fully paid up, the purchaser becomes liable to the company for the payment of the outstanding capital in addition to the previous owner, though in the contractual relationship between the seller and the purchaser only the seller is generally liable. This latter consequence may contradict the intentions of the parties and, if so, they can provide otherwise in the contract.

Finally, it may prove necessary to transfer individual assets, in addition to the shares, in order to acquire the title to the target business as a whole. This is the case where certain assets used in the target business are not owned by the company operating the business but by third parties. In practice it is not unusual, particularly in a family-owned GmbH, that real estate, plant and machinery and industrial property rights are owned by individual shareholders and leased to the company. This may be so for tax reasons or liability reasons or both. Under such circumstances a share purchase transaction will have to be combined with an asset purchase transaction.

(c) Transfer of Shares in Different Types of Company

The distinction under German law between a contractual obligation to transfer and the actual fulfilment of such obligation (as referred to above) also applies when shares are being sold. The form required for the share transfer and the underlying commitment depends on the form of the company concerned.

(1) *Partnership*
The transfer of an interest in a partnership (BGB-Gesellschaft, OHG, KG or GmbH & Co. KG) is effected by transfer agreement between the transferor and the transferee. The transfer generally requires the consent of all partners in order to become effective. Such consent may be given on a case by case basis for individual transactions or on a general basis in the partnership agreement. The partnership agreement may, for instance, provide that interests are freely transferable (which is rarely the case) or that a transfer requires the consent of the majority of the partners (which is quite often the case).

No particular form is required for the transfer agreement, unless the partnership agreement provides otherwise. If, however, the transfer of a partnership interest is effected simultaneously with the transfer of real estate, the transfer agreement requires notarial form. The same holds true for the underlying commitment. If any agreement contains the obligations to transfer both an interest in GmbH & Co. KG and a share in the GmbH being its general partner, the entire agreement requires notarial form in order to be valid. In case this form requirement is not complied with, a subsequent transfer of the share in the GmbH in proper form would retroactively validate ("heal") the agreement, though.

Any change of partners in a commercial partnership (OHG, KG or GmbH & Co. KG) has to be reported to the competent commercial registry for registration. The fulfilment of this reporting requirement does not affect the validity of the change. However, non-compliance may result in continuing liability for the withdrawing partners and unlimited liability of the newly admitted limited partners.

When an interest in a commercial partnership is transferred, the new partner assumes all debts of the partnership, even those created prior to his admission, by operation of law. The liability of the new limited partner is, however, restricted to the nominal amount of his capital interest (*Hafteinlage*) registered in the commercial register and, if such capital interest has been fully paid up and has not been repaid, the new limited partner will not be liable at all, provided that the transfer has been properly notified to the commercial registry.

The withdrawing partner continues to be liable for the debts of the partnership created prior to the registration of his withdrawal in the commercial register. This liability is statute-barred only after five years.

(2) GmbH

The transfer of a share in a GmbH requires an agreement between the transferor and the transferee. The transfer agreement must be recorded by a notary public in order to be valid. This is also true for the underlying commitment to transfer or acquire a share. The requirement of recording extends to all agreements, including side agreements, related to the commitment to transfer or acquire. A commitment not properly recorded will be invalid. However, if the transfer as such is eventually recorded by a notary, the underlying commitment will also be retrospectively validated.

The articles of association may subject a share transfer to restrictions. These may, for example, require the approval of the company, or of some or all of its shareholders, or provide that a share can be transferred only to a party meeting certain qualifications. Moreover, the articles may require that share certificates be delivered though, as a rule, a GmbH does not issue certificates for its shares.

The transfer of the share has to be reported to the GmbH. Notification is not a condition precedent to the validity of the transfer. However, as long as such notification has not been properly made, the GmbH will not recognise the new shareholder as such but will continue to treat the transferor as the shareholder for all purposes.

The share transfer is not registered in any public register in general (see, however, p. 26 for details).

(3) *AG*

Bearer shares (*Inhaberaktien*) are transferred in the same way as moveable assets, i.e. by agreement between the transferor and the transferee and by delivery of the relevant share certificates. No particular form is prescribed for the transfer agreement or for the underlying commitment to transfer and the transfer does not require registration. Normally, the shares are deposited with a bank in which case title can be transferred simply by agreement between the parties without there being any actual delivery of the share certificates.

Registered shares (*Namensaktien*) are transferred by endorsement and agreement and delivery of the relevant share certificates. The articles of association may provide that the transfer also requires the consent of the company itself in order to be valid (so-called restricted registered shares — *vinkulierte Namensaktien*). The transfer of registered shares must be notified to the company and registered in the stock ledger. Failure to notify does not affect the validity of the transfer. However, only a person registered in the stock ledger will be recognised as a shareholder by the AG.

Where no share certificates have been issued (which would not be typical in the case of an AG) the shares are transferred merely by assignment agreement.

(d) Statutory Assumption of Liabilities

A purchaser who acquires all or substantially all of the assets of another natural or legal person becomes liable under s 419 of the Civil Code for such person's obligations existing at the time of acquisition. This statutory assumption of liability may also take place when the purchaser acquires shares in a company, provided he is aware that the shares constitute all or substantially all of the seller's assets (see also p. 60 above). Section 419 of the Civil Code will be abolished effective as from 1st January 1999.

Additional liability may be involuntarily incurred by the purchaser of a share in a GmbH for outstanding capital contributions or by the purchaser of an interest in a limited partnership if the fixed capital contribution of the seller has not been paid up or has been repaid (see pp. 22 and 65 above).

(e) Bona Fide Acquisition

Shares in a company cannot, in general, be acquired by good faith. Moreover, there is no completely reliable way of establishing that the seller is in fact the legal owner of the shares and that the shares are unencumbered. An acquisition may therefore fail because the seller holds no title to the shares or, if it proceeds, the shares may be acquired subject to a pledge.

There is an exception to this rule, in the case of shares in an AG and the shares of the limited partners in a KGaA, if share certificates have been issued. Title to these shares may be acquired (free of encumbrances) by reliance in good faith upon the seller's (unencumbered) ownership or the seller's right of disposition.

(f) Tax Aspects

The tax aspects of a share purchase transaction will be dealt with on pp. 116–119 below.

4. Asset Purchase Transactions compared with Share Purchase Transactions

One of the most critical questions in an acquisition is whether the transaction should be structured as an asset purchase or a share purchase. Each method has its pros and cons both for the seller and the buyer and the appropriate structure will always depend on the specific circumstances and the priorities of the parties. Quite often an advantage for the seller will constitute a disadvantage for the buyer, and vice versa. In some cases the parties will have no choice. The acquisition of a sole proprietorship will always be an asset transaction. The same generally holds true for disposals of parts of a business or of divisions within it and for acquisitions of bankrupt companies. A tender offer by contrast will have to be undertaken by means of a share deal. The major advantages and disadvantages of the two methods of acquisition may be compared from the following overview.

(a) Important Characteristics of Asset Purchase Transactions

The parties are free to select the assets and liabilities to be transferred. On the other hand, the seller may end up with unattractive assets and liabilities and may have to be wound up once it has been stripped of its assets (which will of course involve costs for the seller).

The statutory assumption of unwanted liabilities by the buyer may occur if all or substantially all of the seller's assets are acquired, if the buyer acquires an entire business and continues to use its previous firm name, or if the buyer acquires an entire business or business division.

Tangible assets may be acquired by purchase in good faith.

An asset transaction is more complex and involves more extensive documentation than a share deal (because the assets and liabilities have to be individually specified and individually transferred). The documentation will also have to be notarised if real estate located in Germany or shares in a GmbH are being transferred.

The assets acquired may be used as collateral for financing purposes without posing problems of financial assistance.

The cash flow generated by the assets and liabilities acquired, including any proceeds from the disposals of assets, accrues directly to the buyer without creating problems of financial assistance.

The tax base of the acquired assets may be immediately stepped-up to market value, which generates additional cash flow due to tax savings through increased depreciation or amortisation.

A tax-loss carry-forward (if any) available to the seller will not be available to the buyer.

The seller has to pay capital gains tax (normally at ordinary rates) but he may use existing tax-loss carry-forwards to off-set such capital gains.

The sale of real estate is subject to real estate transfer tax at the rate of 3.5% of the purchase price paid therefor.

Liabilities can only be transferred with the consent of the creditor.

Contracts can only be transferred with the consent of all contract parties. Only contracts of employment transfer automatically, unless the employees object.

Licences and permits under public law cannot, as a rule, be transferred, and have to be applied for anew by the buyer.

It may be difficult or even impossible to transfer the firm name used by the seller.

The works council may have to approve the transaction.

(b) Important Characteristics of Share Purchase Transactions

All assets and liabilities pass with the company the shares of which are transferred. However, this also applies to undisclosed liabilities of the company.

There may be a statutory assumption of the seller's liabilities by the buyer if the shares acquired constitute all or substantially all of the assets of the seller and the buyer is aware of this. In addition, the buyer may become liable for outstanding capital contributions.

Shares may not be acquired by purchase in good faith, unless negotiable share certificates have been issued.

A share purchase deal is a simpler transaction and involves less documentation than an asset purchase deal. No notarisation is necessary, except where shares in a GmbH are acquired or where real estate is purchased in addition to shares.

The use of the assets owned by the acquired company as security for the acquisition financing poses problems of financial assistance.

The cash flow generated by the assets and liabilities of the company acquired, including proceeds from the disposal of assets, accrues to the company itself and the use of such cash flow by the purchaser poses problems of financial assistance.

The book values of the assets owned by the company acquired remain unaffected and, except in the case of partnerships, additional costly steps must be taken to achieve a step-up.

The availability of a tax-loss carry-forward to the company acquired will in general remain unaffected. The carry-forward should therefore be usable by the buyer.

The seller may have to pay capital gains tax only at a privileged rate if he sells shares in a corporation. The sale may even be entirely free of capital gains tax where the seller did not hold more than 25% of the share capital.

If the company owns real estate, real estate transfer tax at a rate of 3.5% will become due only if all shares are acquired by one person or if all shares are acquired by entities belonging to the same group. Even if this is the case the basis for the tax is the assessed tax value of the real estate, which is currently still lower than its fair market value.

Liabilities pass with the company acquired without the need for the consent of creditors.

The contracts of the company acquired remain in force, unless they contain (change of control) break clauses entitling the other party to terminate.

Licences and permits under public law held by the acquired company generally remain unaffected.

The acquisition automatically includes the firm name of the company acquired.

No works council approval is required but the economic committee may have to be informed.

5. Reorganisations and Mergers

(a) General

Germany has fundamentally reformed its law on business reorganisations. A revised Act on Reorganisations (*Umwandlungsgesetz*) came into effect on 1st January 1995.

The primary purpose of the new law is to consolidate and improve the possibilities available for reorganisations of businesses. Prior to the reform, reorganisations had been dealt with in five different statutes which could not always be reconciled with one another. This had resulted in an unsystematic and at times inconsistent legal framework. The Act eliminates these shortcomings by providing a comprehensive codification of the law on reorganisations in one single statute. The Act is not meant to be exhaustive, however, in that certain methods of reorganisation, which had been practised in the past but have not been addressed in the Act, remain available. It may in fact be preferable to use such methods in order to avoid the complexity and risks created by the Act in certain scenarios.

Furthermore, the new law is designed to fill gaps where the former statutes were incomplete. It provides reorganisation techniques which were hitherto unavailable, in particular by introducing the concept of splitting (*Spaltung*) for the first time on a general basis into German corporate law. In addition, the possibility of reorganising is no longer limited to certain company forms but afforded to all entities which are relevant in practice.

Finally, the reform aims at improving the position of both investors and creditors. It is one of the express goals of the legislator to make participations in and commercial dealings with German businesses more transparent, secure and, thereby, more interesting.

Reorganisations are rarely used as an acquisition method, although a merger or consolidation may be appropriate where two companies of comparable size agree on an amalgamation. More frequently, a reorganisation follows an acquisition as a second step in order to combine the entities involved in the transaction, to overcome problems of financial assistance or to achieve tax benefits through a step-up.

(b) Types of Reorganisation

The Act on Reorganisations provides for the following four types of transformation:

(1) Merger or Consolidation (Verschmelzung)
Entities may be combined:

* by transferring the assets and liabilities of one or more entities as a whole to an entity which is already in existence (merger; *Verschmelzung durch Aufnahme*); or
* by transferring the assets and liabilities of two or more entities as a whole to an entity which is newly established (consolidation; *Verschmelzung durch Neugründung*).

In the case of a merger, the assets and liabilities of the merged entities are transferred to the surviving entity by operation of law, the merged entities are dissolved without liquidation and the owners of interests in the merged entities are given interests in the surviving entity. In the case of a consolidation, the assets and liabilities of the constituent entities are transferred to the consolidated entity by operation of law, the constituent entities are dissolved without liquidation and the owners of interests in the constituent entities are given interests in the consolidated entity (Act on Reorganisations, s 2).

(2) Splitting (Spaltung)
Splitting is a technique to separate the assets and liabilities of one entity and to allocate them to different entities. Splitting may be considered as the functional opposite of a merger or consolidation.

The Act authorises three different forms of splitting, namely split-up, split-off and spin-off (s 123). All such forms have in common that assets and liabilities are transferred by operation of law and that the transfer is effected against compensation in the form of interests in the entities acquiring the assets and liabilities so transferred.

In a split-up (*Aufspaltung*) the entity splitting up transfers its assets and liabilities as a whole to two or more already existing or newly established entities. The splitting entity is dissolved without liquidation. The owners of interests in the splitting entity obtain interests in the entities acquiring the assets and liabilities. A split-up is the exact opposite of a merger or consolidation.

In a split-off (*Abspaltung*) the entity splitting off transfers part of its assets and liabilities to one or more already existing or newly established entities. The splitting entity retains a portion of its assets and liabilities and is consequently not dissolved. Again, the owners of interests in the splitting entity obtain interests in the entity or entities acquiring the assets and liabilities. The final result of a split-off is the same as that of a split-up, except that a split-off avoids the transfer of the assets and liabilities retained by the splitting entity and the dissolution of such entity.

In a spin-off (*Ausgliederung*), like in a split-off, the entity spinning off transfers part of its assets and liabilities to one or more already existing or newly established entities, while retaining some of its assets and liabilities. Unlike in the case of a split-off, however, the transferring entity (and not its owners) obtains interests in the entity or entities acquiring the assets and liabilities. The entity acquiring assets and liabilities becomes a subsidiary of the transferring entity. The legal position of the owners of interests in the transferring entity is not affected, although it is clear that their influence regarding the transferred assets becomes mediated.

(3) Transfer of Assets (Vermögensübertragung)

A transfer of assets enables an entity:

* to transfer its assets and liabilities as a whole to an entity already existing and dissolve (as in a merger),
* to transfer its assets and liabilities as a whole to two or more entities already existing and dissolve (as in a split-up), or
* to transfer part of its assets and liabilities to one or more entities already existing (as in a split-off or a spin-off) (Act on Reorganisations, s 174).

In the case of a transfer of assets, contrary to merger and splitting, the compensation for the transferred assets and liabilities may not consist of interests in the acquiring entity but has to take a different form, such as cash. This form of reorganisation is available only to rather few types of entities (e.g. only public law entities and insurance companies can be receiving entities) where, due to the legal structure of some of them, a swap of interests cannot occur.

(4) Change of Legal Form (Formwechsel)

A change of legal form is, as the term suggests, the transformation of the legal form of an entity to a different legal form (s 190). Almost any form of an entity may be reorganised into a different form. A change of legal form does not entail a transfer of assets and liabilities. The legal identity of the entity being transformed is preserved. This holds true even if a partnership is transformed into a corporation and vice versa.

(c) **Reorganisation Procedure**

The reorganisation procedure is highly technical and complex. In general, however, a reorganisation entails the following three basic steps.

First, the participating entities have to enter into an agreement or, if only one entity participates, such entity has to establish a plan of reorganisation. The law provides in great detail for the minimum contents of such agreement or plan.

Second, the owners of interests in the participating entities have to be informed by special written reports about the details of the proposed reorganisation. In many cases the proposed reorganisation is subject to scrutiny by independent experts. On the basis of the information so obtained, the owners decide by resolution on the reorganisation. The resolution must be in notarial form and, in general, requires majorities of at least 75%. Reports and expert examination may be waived if all owners so decide.

Third, the reorganisation has to be registered in the commercial register. It becomes effective only upon its registration.

Dissenting shareholders, employees and creditors affected by a reorganisation are afforded special protection, in particular by tender options and liability provisions. A judicial review of a reorganisation is limited to compliance with formal requirements and, in general, has to be initiated within one month after the respective reorganisation resolution has been passed. In no case can the effectiveness of a reorganisation be challenged on the grounds that the conversion ratio or compensation for the interests affected has been improperly determined. An owner of interests who feels disadvantaged in this regard can only sue in special proceedings for additional cash compensation (so-called *Spruchverfahren*).

(d) **Tax Aspects**

The revised Act on Reorganisations has been supplemented by a new Act on Taxation of Reorganisations, which also came into effect on 1st January 1995.

The new Act on Taxation of Reorganisations is designed to remove existing tax impediments in cases where legally permissible reorganisations are desirable for commercial reasons. It increases the possibilities of reorganising businesses in a tax-neutral manner and transferring loss carry-forwards in the reorganisation process. The new tax law allows corporations to be reorganised into corporations, partnerships to be reorganised into partnerships, partnerships to be reorganised into corporations, partnerships to be split, and what is new, corporations to be reorganised into partnerships and corporations to be split, all at book value, i.e. income tax free.

The introduction of the possibility of reorganising a corporation into a partnership at book value has also resulted in improvements in the M&A field. In cases where the shares in a German corporation are bought and the book values of its assets are considerably lower than the purchase price for the shares, the buyer wants to replace the non-depreciable shares by depreciable assets, thus creating additional depreciation potential. In the past, the step-up has been achieved by a combined share and assets purchase transaction, where the buyer first bought the shares and then entered into an internal asset deal. This model has the drawback, however, that it results in a trade tax cost and, possibly, timing difficulties. The new law provides the opportunity to carry out a step-up without these disadvantages if the buyer reorganises the acquired corporation into a partnership (OHG, KG or GmbH & Co. KG).

6. Takeovers and Tender Offers

(a) General

The term "takeover" has become commonly used to describe the acquisition of a majority interest in a target company which may or may not be based on prior agreement with the management of that company. Typically, the target company is a corporation.

One of the crucial issues in a takeover will normally be the question of what level of shareholding will need to be acquired in order to obtain control. As mentioned above, the necessary level of majority and the rights such majority affords will largely depend on the legal form of the target and its articles of association. As a rule, the takeover both of an AG and a GmbH should result in the acquisition of a majority holding of at least 75% of the share capital. This majority is required for certain basic corporate transactions which may become necessary after the takeover, such as changes to the articles of association, increases and reductions of the share capital, the disposal of all or a substantial part of the business, the entering into profit transfer agreements and control agreements, reorganisations and liquidations. Since attendance at shareholders' meetings of large AGs is never 100% (for AGs listed on a stock exchange it ranges between 50 and 80%), the acquisition of about 50% of all the existing voting shares may often result in the required 75% majority at the shareholders' meeting being obtained. Because the disclosure obligations for holdings in listed corporations have been considerably expanded, a secret accumulation of substantial interests ("creeping-in") will no longer be possible.*

The management of a company acquiring another company will have to make sure that they have the requisite authority to do so. If the acquiror is a German corporation, it may well be the case that its articles require the management to obtain the consent of the supervisory board or (in the case of a GmbH) the shareholders' meeting before making an acquisition. According to a quite startling decision of the Federal Supreme Court the management of a stock corporation has to obtain the prior consent of the shareholders' meeting for any major structural change of the corporation, and a major acquisition might qualify as such (Federal Supreme Court, decision of 25th February 1982, BGHZ 83, 122 ("*Holzmüller*")). On the other hand, even if the management does not obtain any necessary internal consents, the actions taken on behalf of the corporation are normally legally valid and binding nevertheless. An exception may apply if the other party has actual knowledge that the management acts *ultra vires*.

A takeover may be effected by a privately negotiated share transaction with one or several major shareholders. In the case of an AG having listed shares, the acquisition may also be effected by purchases on the stock exchanges. This type of transaction is regularly handled through a bank.

Another means of effecting a takeover is a public tender offer. This may be mandatory or voluntary.

Mandatory tender offers are those offers which must be made in accordance with corporate law under specific circumstances. Such mandatory tender offers are generally required to be made to outside shareholders, e.g. in cases of control agreements and profit transfer agreements, short mergers and other reorganisations (Stock Corporation Act, ss 305, 320 and Act on Reorganisations, ss 207 and 29, respectively). As a rule, mandatory tender offers are not used to acquire control. Rather,

---

*Reporting thresholds at 5%, 10%, 25%, 50% and 75% of the voting rights (see p. 33 *et seq.* above).

they are a legal consequence of corporate measures taken by a shareholder already holding a controlling interest.

A *voluntary tender offer* may be defined as a non-mandatory public offer made by a bidder to all holders of a class of shares to acquire all or a specified portion of their shares for a fixed cash consideration or in exchange for other securities and which is held open for a specified period of time. Voluntary tender offers are not governed by any specific statutory rules and to date, only the non-mandatory Takeover Code applies. The Takeover Code aims at the protection of the target shareholders by ensuring their equal and fair treatment, by affording them an adequate period for deliberation on the basis of a detailed offer and by preventing manipulations of the market price. Details have been explained on pp. 37–43 above. Although the Code only constitutes recommendations, it will generally have to be complied with in practice.

(b) Barriers to Takeovers

Voluntary tender offers cannot be considered a common takeover device in Germany. Indeed, during the period from 1981 to 1988, there were only 29 cases. The number of voluntary tender offers jumped to about 250 for the period from 1989 to mid-1995. In most of these cases, however, the goal of the offer was not to aquire control. Hostile takeover attempts are quite rare, although on the rise. The US and British takeover battles have no equivalent in the German market.

The main reason for this is certainly the limited number of targets. Although all company forms (e.g. AG, KGaA, GmbH, OHG, KG) may theoretically constitute a takeover target, a tender offer is likely to be successful only if made in respect of corporations whose shares are both listed on a stock exchange and widely spread. However, there are only about 810 German corporations listed on a German stock exchange, a large number of which are in turn affiliated with other companies, i.e. not really publicly held. Notwithstanding the increasing number of listings in recent years, it is estimated that the number of candidates suitable for a tender offer does currently not exceed about 100.

Moreover, the low popularity of tender offers is due to some additional idiosyncrasies of the German corporate environment.

(1) *Identification of Shareholders*
The identification of shareholders may be difficult. The vast majority of German AGs issue bearer shares. There is no share register which would identify the owners of such shares. The situation is only different

with regard to substantial shareholders. A person acquiring 5, 10, 25, 50 or 75 of the voting rights of a stock corporation must notify the corporation of the acquisition which in turn is required to publish such notice (see p. 33 *et seq.* above). A potential acquirer, therefore, can ascertain the ownership structure and the identity of substantial shareholders, but not that of shareholders with interests below 5%. Access to the "small" shareholders is possible only through the media and, once a bid has been launched, through depositary banks. If a bidder publishes its bid in a special legal gazette (*Wertpapier-Mitteilungen*), the German banks depositing shares are obliged under their uniform general business terms to notify their shareholders–depositors thereof (No. 39 General Business Terms of Banks).

(2) *Management Control*
The acquisition of a majority interest in an AG does not automatically result in management control. The company is managed and represented by its management board whose authorities are broad and encompassing. They range from day-to-day management to the taking and implementation of fundamental corporate policy and strategy decisions. The shareholders' meeting or individual shareholders may not give instructions to the management board or otherwise interfere with its activities. Management control may be obtained only when the purchaser replaces the members of the management board by its "own" people, but this may turn out to be a difficult and time-consuming process.

The members of the management board are appointed and removed by the supervisory board. The appointment is normally for the maximum period of five years. Staggered appointments are customary. During the term of office, a member of the management board can only be removed for cause, such as a gross violation of duties, incompetence or a vote of no confidence by the shareholders' meeting for reasons which are not manifestly arbitrary. A removal is deemed to be effective until its ineffectiveness has been determined by a final and unappealable court decision, which may take years (Stock Corporation Act, s 84, para 3, sentence 4). The supervisory board decides normally by simple majority. If the company employs 2000 or more persons, 50% of the supervisory board members are employee-elected and resolutions require a two-thirds majority in the first ballot. Only if this majority is not attained and after a conciliation committee has been involved will simple majority suffice, the chairman of the supervisory board (who is shareholder-elected) having a tie-breaking second vote. In order to replace members of the management board, the purchaser therefore must first get enough of his confidants on the supervisory board and cause must exist if the replacement shall take place during the term of office.

Depending on the applicable co-determination law, up to 50% of the supervisory board members are employee-elected. The other supervisory board members are elected by the shareholders' meeting or, if the articles so provide, designated by individual shareholders. Members of the supervisory board usually serve for the maximum term of about five years and their terms may be staggered. The shareholder-elected members may be removed at any time prior to the expiration of their term of office by shareholders' resolution. Such a resolution requires a majority of three-quarters of the votes cast, unless the articles let a simple majority suffice (which is not often the case). The shareholder designated members may be removed at any time by the shareholders entitled to the nomination right. The employee-elected members cannot be removed by the shareholders.

The foregoing illustrates the legal obstacles a replacement of the management board may face. The purchaser first has to gain control of the supervisory board, but the employee representatives on the board are out of reach for him and for the replacement of the shareholder representatives he normally needs a majority of three-quarters of the votes cast in the shareholders' meeting. Even if the purchaser succeeds in replacing all shareholder representatives, he may find it difficult to oust the existing management for factual reasons because the labour side is often conservative and apprehensive of change.

(3) *Protection of Corporation*
A stock corporation is protected in various ways against undue influence by its shareholders (see p. 23 *et seq.* above):

- If a controlling shareholder influences an AG to take or not to take certain actions and this results in a disadvantage for the controlled AG, the shareholder has to indemnify the corporation. Compliance with this rule is policed by the so-called "dependency report" (*Abhängigkeitsbericht*) which has to be prepared annually by the controlled AG, audited by its accountants and examined by its supervisory board. The dependency report must list the transactions between the AG and its parent and state whether or not the AG has been disadvantaged.
- A majority shareholder (with a majority of at least 75% of the capital represented at a shareholders' meeting) could enter into a control agreement with the corporation which would provide him with the right to manage and control such corporation and give

even disadvantageous instructions. This would come at a price, however. Mandatory law requires the controlling shareholder to compensate the controlled corporation for any annual net loss. Furthermore, entering into a control agreement would entitle the minority shareholders to a dividend guarantee and appraisal rights (Stock Corporation Act, s 302 *et seq.*).

- If a shareholder intentionally uses its influence to induce board members or certain key employees to act to the company's detriment, the company, and possibly other shareholders, may claim damages (s 117).

- An AG must not repay contributions to the shareholders (s 57). All payments to shareholders other than declared dividend payments, payments following a reduction of the registered share capital and payments in the course of arm's-length commercial transactions are, in general, prohibited. Even interim dividends during the course of the business year are illegal (s 59). The same is true for financial or commercial benefits granted by the company to any of its shareholders. Section 71a of the Stock Corporation Act makes it expressly illegal that an AG grants a loan to a third party or secures a loan taken up by a third party for the purpose of financing the acquisition of shares in the AG. These rules make financial assistance by a target company in the form of an AG practically impossible.

(4) *Protection of Minority Shareholders*

The rules protecting the corporation protect minority shareholders as well. But there are some additional concepts of law which are more specifically designed to safeguard the interests of minority shareholders:

- It is a statutory requirement that all shareholders of a corporation be treated equally (s 53a). No shareholder, including a purchaser of shares, may request or be granted any preferential treatment. The management board of the corporation is under a legal obligation to comply with this rule which may be quite welcome at times when the board faces an unfriendly takeover situation.

- A shareholder owes certain fiduciary duties (*Treuepflichten*) both to the company and its fellow shareholders (see p. 23 above).

- There is, in general, no possibility of acquiring the interests of minority shareholders by statutory mergers or rights of compulsory acquisition without giving the minority shareholder the right to become a shareholder in the majority shareholder. Minority shareholders may be squeezed out if the majority shareholder dissolves the corporation (which requires a shareholders' resolution passed with 75% of the share capital represented at the meeting) and purchases its business in the following liquidation. However, the sale of the business to the majority shareholder must not be pre-agreed and has to be effected at arm's length and the difference between book value of the business and its market value will be subject to income tax, which will normally make a liquidation unattractive. A better method to get rid of minority shareholders might be to transform the corporation into a partnership under the new Act on Reorganisations and thereafter terminate the partnership and have its assets and liabilities accrue with its general partner (the majority shareholder of the former corporation) in a tax neutral way. This latter method has not yet been tested in the courts, however, and might appear rather aggressive.

- Each shareholder is entitled to challenge shareholders' resolutions and (within limits) to have corporate reorganisations reviewed by the courts. This may prove cumbersome, costly and time-consuming for a purchaser.

(5) *Role of Banks*

Finally, an unfriendly bidder may well encounter resistance from the major German banks. German banks exercise substantial influence on stock corporations. They often own large portions of shares themselves and have representatives sitting on the supervisory board. Most shares of smaller shareholders are deposited with German banks who vote them by way of proxy (Stock Corporation Act, s 135). In practice, the proxy process authorises the banks to vote deposited shares in accordance with their own proposals. It is estimated that the five largest banks in Germany own about 15% of the country's listed shares and that the banks control an additional 20% by way of proxy votes. Last but not least, German companies rely considerably on debt finance and the banks are often the largest creditors of the target.

For these reasons it is unlikely that tender offers in Germany will ever reach a volume comparable to that in the US or Great Britain. Nevertheless, the increased activities on the merger and acquisitions market in general, the involvement of leading German corporations in tender offers abroad and an increasingly widespread acceptance of hostile takeovers in the German business community will certainly have a stimulating impact on the German takeover scene.

(c) **Defensive Tactics**

In anticipation of hostile takeovers, a number of large corporations have started to prepare defensive measures like those implemented by some companies in the 1970s to protect themselves against major petrodollar investments. The defensive arsenal available under German law is quite limited, though. Many of the defensive tactics frequently encountered in the US, such as the repurchase by the company of its own shares, the issuance of "poison pill" securities and the grant of "golden parachutes", are not permissible in Germany. Hostile takeovers may turn out to be difficult, time-consuming and costly but the obstacles created by and permissible under German law are by no means insurmountable.

The introduction of most of the defences available in Germany necessitates a shareholders' resolution. This is true in particular where the creation of the defence requires an amendment of the articles of association. Typically, for an amendment of the articles a majority of 75% of the capital represented at the shareholders' meeting and a simple majority of the votes present are required (Stock Corporation Act, s 179, para 2, s 133, para 1). The 75% capital requirement may in general be changed by the articles of association to a greater or lower majority (s 179, para 2, sentence 2).

Where defensive measures are created by shareholders' vote, they may also be eliminated by the shareholders, normally with the same majorities as required for their creation. In general, it is therefore ultimately the shareholders' meeting who decides on the success of a takeover attempt.

The afore-mentioned majority requirements are somewhat misleading, however. Because shareholders' meetings of public corporations have usually a low attendance rate, a shareholder who holds for instance 35% of the outstanding shares often has a simple majority in the shareholders' meeting. A statutory quorum does not exist. The articles could provide for a quorum but this is not customary in practice because it might necessitate time-consuming and costly repetitions of meetings. A 35% shareholder may therefore be well in a position to change the articles of association if they let simple majority suffice for a change.

There is not much the management board can do against a takeover attempt. The shareholders are the economic owners of the corporation. They decide on the sale of the corporation or its liquidation. It is not for the management to influence the structure of the shareholding in the corporation.

The rights and obligations of the management board in a takeover situation have not yet been defined. According to the prevailing view in legal literature, the management is subject to an obligation of neutrality. The Takeover Code has established the rule that once a tender offer has been launched, the management may not take any measures that are contrary to the interests of the shareholders (article 19). This does not prevent the management from commenting on the offer. On the contrary, the management should evaluate the offer both economically and legally and inform the shareholders of its findings (article 18). For extreme and rare cases (e.g. offer by "Mafia" organisations or illegal financing) some legal authors want to make an exception from the principle of neutrality and allow the board to take defensive measures. It appears to be doubtful, however, whether such an exception is necessary. The corporation, its shareholders, its employees and its creditors are protected by a host of statutory provisions and principles. No action by the management board is normally required to safeguard their interests. When the management board raises defences against a takeover, the prima facie assumption is always that the board pursues no other interests than its own.

In no case can the management change the articles in order to resist a hostile takeover. It may only call a shareholders' meeting and suggest changes to the shareholders. This is a time-consuming process which is often no longer practicable once a tender offer has been launched.

The following are the most common tactics that are considered in the defence against unfriendly bids:

(1) *Limitation of Voting Rights (Höchststimmrecht)*
The articles of association of a corporation can provide that the voting rights attributable to the shares of a single shareholder are limited to a specific ceiling (say 5% or 10% of all votes), regardless of the size of the interest held (Stock Corporation Act, s 134, para 1, sentence 2). A considerable number of German stock corporations, among them prestigious industrial companies and financial institutions, have established such maximum voting rights. In order to avoid circumventions, voting right limitations are typically supplemented by clauses in the articles providing that shares held by affiliates or trustees of a shareholder are attributed to such shareholder.

A limitation of voting rights does not make the corporation immune to a takeover, however. An acquirer might try to group other non-affiliated shareholders around him in order to vote in concert or to gain their support to abolish the limitation. An even more promising approach for a potential acquirer would be to launch a tender offer which is contingent on a prior abolishment of the voting right limitation by the shareholders. The elimination of the voting right limitation requires a shareholders' resolution with a majority of 75% of the share capital represented at the meeting and a simple majority of the votes present thereat. The articles may provide that a simple majority of both the share capital and the votes represented at the meeting suffice. If the offered price reflects an attractive premium, one can normally expect the shareholders to eliminate the restriction on voting rights and sell their shares.

Voting restrictions have come under attack in the business community. Moreover, the EU Commission plans to dispense with the ability to limit the votes of a single shareholder. The amended proposal for a Fifth Council directive of 20th November 1991 follows the "one share one vote" principle and permits voting restrictions only for preference shares (shares carrying special pecuniary advantages) which must not be issued for an amount exceeding 50% of the subscribed capital.

(2) *Restricted Registered Shares (Vinkulierte Namensaktien)*
The articles of association of a corporation can provide that the issued shares are registered shares (*Namensaktien*) and that any share transfer requires the approval of the corporation in order to be effective (*vinkulierte Namensaktien*) (Stock Corporation Act, s 68, para 2). The approval is granted by the management board unless the articles provide that the supervisory board or the shareholders' meeting is to decide. The articles may specify the reasons for which the approval may be denied. Absent any exhaustive specifications, the management board (or, if the articles so provide, the supervisory board or the shareholders' meeting) has broad discretion when deciding on the approval of a proposed share transfer.

The issuance of restricted registered shares has a long-standing tradition. Originally, this type of shares was used by smaller family-owned companies in order to keep the composition of the shareholders under control or, more precisely, to refuse admission of outsiders not welcome to the founding family. More recently, restricted registered shares have received a broader application and developed into a general anti-takeover device. However, if the original articles of the corporation do not already provide for restricted registered shares, it is quite difficult, if not impossible, to create them later on because such a change would require the consent of each single shareholder affected (in addition to the majority necessary for a change of the articles) (Stock Corporation Act, s 180, para 2). A conversion of shares into restricted registered shares would limit their marketability considerably and it is not likely that a substantial number of shareholders would be in favour of such a change. This is why restricted registered shares are rarely seen in large public corporations, with the exception of insurance companies.

If a potential acquirer cannot convince the target company to give the necessary approval for the acquisition, he may try to gain control by entering into trust agreements with registered shareholders who continue to be shareholders of record, but exercise all their rights subject to the instructions and for the benefit of the "acquirer". Trust agreements of this kind are considered as a circumvention of the approval requirement. These agreements are not enforceable and votes cast in consummating them are probably invalid, provided that their existence can be proved. Again, a better method for the would-be acquirer is to make a tender offer which is contingent on the elimination of the transfer restriction in the articles of association. The necessary change of the articles requires a shareholders' resolution passed with a majority of 75% of the share capital represented at the meeting and a simple majority of the votes present thereat. If the articles so provide, a simple majority of both the share capital and the votes represented at the meeting suffice.

(3) Authorised Capital (Genehmigtes Kapital)
The shareholders can amend the articles of association to the effect that the board of management is authorised for a period of up to five years to increase the share capital and issue new shares (so-called "authorised capital"; *genehmigtes Kapital*). The increase must not exceed 50% of the existing share capital and new shares shall be issued only with the consent of the supervisory board. Such an amendment of the articles would require a majority of at least 75% of the capital represented at the shareholders' meeting and a simple majority of the votes present thereat (Stock Corporation Act, s 202).

The authorised capital might be used to sell new shares to a third party considered to be more disposed towards management, a so-called "white knight". New shares can be sold to third parties, however, only if and to the extent the statutory pre-emptive rights of the existing shareholders have been excluded or have not been exercised. An exclusion of the shareholders' pre-emptive rights is quite difficult under German law. It requires a shareholders' resolution with at least a majority of 75% of the share capital represented at the vote and adequate justification. The creation of a takeover barrier has not been considered as an adequate justification so far. Under a recent amendment of the statute the exclusion of the statutory pre-emptive right is deemed permissible if the offering price for the new shares is not substantially below the stock exchange price and if the capital increase does not exceed 10% of the company's registered share capital (Stock Corporation Act, s 186, para 3, sentence 4). Within these latter limitations, the issuance of new shares might serve as a takeover defence but the management board would have to proceed with extreme caution in order not to violate its fiduciary duties towards the company.

(4) *Acquisition of own Shares*
It is a basic rule of German corporate law that an AG may not acquire its own shares (Stock Corporation Act, s 71). Exceptions are permitted merely for a limited number of specific cases. The only exception which might be considered in the context of a takeover is that which allows the acquisition of the corporation's own shares "if the acquisition is necessary in order to avert severe and imminent danger from the corporation" (s 71, para 1, No. 1). It is quite settled that this exception cannot be relied on in order to ward off an unwelcome acquirer, although some legal writers suggest applying it in "extreme cases".

Even if an acquisition of own shares was permissible, the corporation might never acquire more than an aggregate of 10% of its shares, the acquisition price must be paid out of free funds and the corporation might not exercise any rights, in particular voting rights, attributable to its own shares (s 71b). For these reasons at least the acquisition of own shares by the corporation cannot be considered a suitable takeover impediment.

(5) *Disposition of Assets*
A target corporation might consider disposing of important assets ("crown jewels") in order to make itself less attractive to a raider. This could involve the sale of subsidiaries by way of private agreement or flotation or the sale of major parts of the business.

In principle, the sale of assets of the company falls within the authority of the management board. The articles or the supervisory board may require that the sale of important assets has to be approved by the supervisory board. This principle is subject to two critical limitations.

First, the management board has to act in the best interest of the corporation. Only under exceptional circumstances may a sale of important business assets motivated by the desire to avoid a change of control be justifiable under such test. The management board faces the risk of personal liability for damages suffered by the corporation if its actions are found to be not in the corporation's best interest.

Second, a landmark decision passed by the Federal Supreme Court in 1982 has restricted the authority of the management board when major portions of a business or an entire division are being spun off. According to this decision the management board is required to obtain the prior approval of the shareholders' meeting in all cases where the board wants to carry out a decision which has such a significant impact on the company or the rights and interests of its shareholders that the board cannot reasonably assume that it is entitled to take such decision exclusively on its own responsibility (BGHZ 83, 122 (*"Holzmüller"*)). The exact scope and consequences of this decision are still under discussion but it seems to be quite clear that the sale of crown jewels, if at all permissible, would have to be approved by the shareholders' meeting.

(6) Changes in Ownership; Cross-holdings
The management of the target company may try to thwart an unfriendly takeover attempt by finding a purchaser which it considers as friendly ("white knight"). This is not objectionable so long as the management of the target company is not promised any monetary or other financial advantages to be paid out of the assets of the target. The introduction of a competing offerer is clearly in the interest of the shareholders.

Another protection against takeovers can be achieved by cross-holdings where two companies acquire interests in each other. Simple cross-holdings are widely used and legally permissible. Cross-holdings exceeding 25% (*wechselseitige Beteiligungen*) are subject to certain restrictions as far as the exercise of shareholder rights is concerned (Stock Corporation Act, ss 19, 328). The creation of qualified cross-holdings, i.e. the acquisition of an interest by a corporation in the controlling parent company is subject to the same severe restrictions as the acquisition of own shares by the corporation. This means in particular that it is not permissible in order to establish a takeover barrier (s 71d, sentence 2).

7. Leveraged Buy-Outs and Management Buy-Outs

(a) Introduction

The term *leveraged buy-out* (LBO) describes the acquisition of a business where the acquisition is funded primarily by debt and only to a limited extent by equity. Typically, the debt will be serviced out of the profit, cash flow and assets of the acquired entity and, to the extent possible, the debt will also be secured on the assets of the target.

A *management buy-out* (MBO) is the acquisition of a business by a group of investors including members of the existing management of that business. In Germany, as in the US, most of the MBOs can also be categorised as LBOs, because they are highly geared with debt.

There are no reliable figures on the numbers of leveraged transactions actually implemented in Germany because most of these transactions, in particular in the medium-size range, are not made public. It is safe to say, however, that in Germany the market for LBOs and MBOs is still considerably less developed than in the USA or the UK. On the other hand, the potential market in Germany for leveraged transactions is certainly substantial. There are thousands of small and medium-sized companies which will face succession problems when the postwar generation that founded such companies wishes to withdraw. A substantial number of conglomerates wish to sell off divisions or subsidiaries as they revert to their "core business". Managers have become aware of buy-out opportunities, leveraged transactions are accepted in the business community and the funds and know-how necessary for such transactions are available. Financing specialists expect the flow of transactions in Germany to increase considerably.

(b) Financing Structure

Leveraged transactions require a specific financing mix. The financing must in general terms be realistic in the light of the projected cash flow capacity of the target, must leave the target sufficient flexibility and must provide the equity investors and debt providers with adequate returns for the risks they are taking.

In MBOs, the capital structure will also depend on the degree of ownership control the managers wish or can afford to have. The outside investors usually expect the managers to make an investment which constitutes a suitably appreciable risk for them. The knowledge that they have risked their personal finances to a considerable degree should maximise the management's performance and enhance its commitment to the success of the venture.

Leveraged transactions normally involve three levels of finance, namely equity, senior debt and mezzanine debt. Each financing level has different risks and, therefore, different expectations of returns. In a typical transaction in Germany, the financing would be made up as to 10 to 20% in the form of equity, as to 10 to 20% in the form of mezzanine debt and as to the balance in the form of senior debt.

(1) *Equity*

Equity will be provided by the investors, who may include financial institutions, venture capital companies, specialised LBO funds and other institutional investors. In an MBO, the management will normally wish to participate as much as possible in the equity. However, there are relatively few buy-outs in Germany where the management has obtained a majority of the equity. The equity portion acquired by the management is usually paid for out of its own resources but is often borrowed from a bank.

If management pays less than the other investors for an equal percentage of the equity because the other investors pay premiums over par, or if management is granted options to increase its percentage of the equity at a later date, e.g. depending on the achievement of financial targets, this may result in a tax liability for the management.

(2) Senior Debt
Senior debt is usually financed by a bank or a syndicate of banks. It may be secured or unsecured. Typically, however, the lender looks to have security over substantially all the assets directly or indirectly acquired.

Senior debt quite often takes the form of a term loan. In practice, the loan may range between seven and ten years and the banks will probably require half of the credit to be repaid when half of the term has expired. The term loan may sometimes be supplemented by a short-term working capital facility.

(3) Mezzanine Debt
German law offers a variety of forms of mezzanine finance, such as subordinated loans, profit-sharing loans (partiarische Darlehen), silent partnership (stille Gesellschaft), corporate profit participation rights (Genussrechte), various types of bonds and seller's notes. It is unusual in Germany to issue subordinated bonds — also known as "junk bonds" — as a form of mezzanine debt. This may be largely attributable to the fact that, until the end of 1990, the issue of negotiable debt instruments generally required the prior approval of the Federal Ministry of Economics. Such approval was only granted if the credit standing of the issuer was beyond reasonable doubt, a requirement hardly ever fulfilled in a leveraged transaction. The approval requirement has been replaced in the meantime by an obligation on the part of the issuer to publish a prospectus. But in spite of this technical facilitation of bond financing and notwithstanding the expected growth of the LBO market, it is not likely that this financing method will play a significant role in the near future. The reservations in the minds of the public against subordinated bonds, fuelled by the collapse of the US junk bond market in the late 80s, seem to be too strong to be overcome for the time being.

At present, mezzanine finance for acquisitions regularly takes the form of subordinated loans. The terms of subordination are a matter for negotiation between the borrower and the various providers of debt. The senior lenders will usually permit interest payments on the subordinated loans but are likely to require that repayment of principal should only start after the senior debt has been fully repaid. In bankruptcy or liquidation proceedings, the subordinated lender will have a claim even if the senior lenders are not repaid, but he will have to turn over any proceeds received by him to the senior lenders to the extent necessary to make good any shortfalls in the senior debt repayment. Subordinated loans are typically unsecured. Because of their higher risk, subordinated lenders will generally charge interest at considerably higher rates than senior lenders.

(4) *Equity-Replacing Loans with an "Equity Kicker"*
A particular problem may arise when equity and debt are provided by the same person. A loan made by a shareholder to his company may be considered "equity-replacing" if granted when the company is in financial difficulty. The test to be used is whether the company would have obtained the loan in question on arm's-length market conditions from an unrelated third party. If the answer is negative, the loan is classified as equity-replacing. It is certainly conceivable that a shareholder loan made in a highly leveraged buy-out would fall within the category of equity-replacing loans.

Repayment of an equity-replacing loan is subject to restrictions which depend on the legal nature of the borrower and whether the claim for repayment is made prior to or during bankruptcy (or composition proceedings for the avoidance of bankruptcy). In essence, the applicable restrictions result in a subordination of the shareholder loan. For example, during bankruptcy or composition proceedings of a GmbH, the shareholder lender cannot require repayment of an equity-replacing loan. The loan is treated as share capital and any security provided therefor by the company cannot be realised.

A shareholder loan may also be given by a future shareholder. If a lender in a buy-out transaction is granted an option to acquire shares in the borrowing company ("equity kicker"), the loan is likely to be categorised as a shareholder loan and, depending on the circumstances, may also be equity-replacing.

Because of these risks, some financial institutions have decided not to provide equity and debt at the same time and to refrain from taking any form of "equity kicker" when they grant debt finance.

(c) **Structure of Transaction**

Leveraged buy-out transactions are "normal" acquisitions involving considerations common to all takeovers. However, the particular financing technique characterising an LBO poses some additional problems for the structure of the transaction.

(1) *Acquisition Vehicle*

The acquisition of the target business is generally effected through a corporation newly established by the investors (*NewCo*). Because of its flexibility, the GmbH is the preferred form of incorporation. This method of acquisition has various advantages. Among other things, it helps to avoid personal liability which the investors might incur under different concepts of German law, were they to acquire the target business directly. Moreover, the acquisition through a corporation offers tax advantages since a later resale of shares of such corporation by managers holding not more than 25% of the capital is tax-free.

(2) *Asset or Share Transaction?*

As referred to above, a crucial question in any acquisition is whether to buy assets or shares. Whereas each type of transaction has its usual pros and cons from both the seller's and the buyer's perspective, particular care must be taken to ensure that two key requirements of a leveraged buy-out can be satisfied. First, it must be permissible to use the cash flow and the assets of the target business to service and secure the debt incurred by NewCo for its acquisition. Second, the cash flow available must be as high as possible.

In an asset purchase transaction the fulfilment of the above-mentioned requirements does not pose any particular problems. The target business becomes part of NewCo. Both its assets and cash flow — which now belong to NewCo — may be used by NewCo for the purposes of servicing and securing its debt. To the extent that the purchase price for the target business exceeds its aggregate book values, the assets may be revalued to their market value and any remaining balance may be attributed to goodwill. This results in increased cash flow due to tax savings through higher depreciation or amortisation. Where available, the "assets" type deal is an ideal structure for a leveraged transaction. However, for tax reasons the sellers will usually prefer the sale of shares if they are individuals or foreign corporations.

Things are more difficult in a share purchase transaction. This is due to the capital preservation rules under German law. These rules, in general, severely restrict the financial assistance that can be given by the target in connection with the acquisition of its shares. Furthermore, a share deal leaves the book values of the assets of the target company unaffected and does not generate higher cash flow, at least when the shares in a corporation are acquired. It is, of course, possible to pledge the shares in the target company to the lenders as security. However, this is not satisfactory since a pledge over the shares ranks after the creditors of the target.

(3) *Capital Preservation Rules*
The capital preservation rules to be complied with when shares or interests in a company are acquired will vary according to the legal form of the target. They may be summarised as follows:

(i) Stock Corporation — AG
Under s 57 of the Stock Corporation Act, an AG must not repay contributions to the shareholders. All payments to shareholders other than declared dividend payments and payments in the course of arm's-length commercial transactions are, in general, prohibited by this provision. The prohibition not only covers outright payments to shareholders, but also extends to any financial or commercial benefits, including upstream guarantees and other collateral for loans taken up by a shareholder. Furthermore, under s 71a of the Stock Corporation Act, an AG must not grant a loan to a third party or secure a loan taken up by a third party for the purpose of financing the acquisition of shares in the AG. A violation of these prohibitions may result in the invalidity of the transaction in question, may have negative tax consequences and may entail personal, civil and even criminal liability on the part of the management involved. This makes financial assistance by an AG practically impossible. Moreover, where there are any minority shareholders, the principle of equal treatment (*Gleich-behandlungsgebot*) will prohibit financial assistance for the benefit of the majority without the consent of the minority shareholders.

(ii) Company with Limited Liability — GmbH
Section 30 of the GmbH Act prohibits any payments by a GmbH to its shareholders pursuant to which the net book assets of the company would be reduced to a level below the subscribed share capital. This prohibition against repayment of share capital is being broadly interpreted. It applies to the granting of benefits which have any financial or commercial value, including upstream guarantees and other collateral. Therefore, any financial assistance by a GmbH must be limited to the amount by which the net book equity exceeds the subscribed share capital. When security is provided, the test must be made twice, namely, when the security is granted and when it is

realised. A violation of s 30 of the GmbH Act may also have the legal consequences referred to above.

Even if s 30 of the GmbH Act is not violated, there are two other problem areas to be considered. First, any contribution by the GmbH to its shareholders must comply with the principle of equal treatment (*Gleichbehandlungsgebot*). In practice this means that financial assistance will not be possible if there are any minority shareholders of the target company whose shares have not been acquired. Second, the Federal Supreme Court has held in two decisions that the management of the GmbH may be subject to criminal liability for breach of fiduciary duties (*Untreue*) under s 266 of the Criminal Code (*Strafgesetzbuch*) if it makes or allows payments through the company which either jeopardise the liquidity or existence of the company or which are "in violation of the principles of an orderly businessman". The broad and unspecific language of these decisions has substantially increased the risks surrounding financial assistance, in particular in highly leveraged transactions.

(iii) General Partnership — OHG and Limited Partnership — KG

The law on partnerships does not provide for specific capital preservation rules. Partnerships are, however, governed by the principle of equal treatment. This has the practical result that financial assistance by a partnership is only feasible where all of its interests are acquired.

Moreover, in the case of the acquisition of a KG, the return to the limited partners of their registered capital contribution results in their assuming personal liability for the debts of the company. This liability is limited, however, to the amount of their registered capital contribution. Any financial benefit provided from the assets of the company, including the granting of security, will be considered as a return of the registered capital contributions. In addition, in the case of the acquisition of a GmbH & Co. KG, the capital preservation rule of s 30 of the GmbH Act has to be complied with.

(4) *Refined Concepts for Share Transactions*

The capital preservation rules of German law make financial assistance by AGs, GmbHs and KGs risky, if not impossible. It is not surprising that those involved in the practice of buy-outs have felt aggrieved with this situation. Structures have, therefore, been developed in order to overcome the financial assistance problems outlined above and to create at the same time increased cash flow at the level of NewCo. The most popular concepts work, broadly speaking, as follows:

(i) Merger Model
This model is used when the target acquired by NewCo is a corporation.

NewCo acquires the shares in the target company. Immediately thereafter, the target company is merged into NewCo (upstream merger). This makes the cash flow and assets of the target company directly available to NewCo.

However, this solution has substantial disadvantages. First, the creditors of the merged company may ask for security. Second, if the book values of the assets of the target are revalued upwards to their market value for tax purposes, the revaluation increase is fully taxable. Due to its disadvantages, the merger model will only in exceptional cases be an attractive solution to meet the requirements of a leveraged transaction.

(ii) Combination Model
This model is also used when the target acquired by NewCo is a corporation.

NewCo acquires the shares in the target company. Immediately thereafter, NewCo purchases by means of an internal asset deal the assets and liabilities of the target at their fair market value, which is equivalent to the price paid for the shares. The profit realised by the target company, including any reserves, is distributed as a dividend to NewCo. Then Newco writes down the value of its investment in the target company by an amount equal to the dividend distribution (*ausschüttungsbedingte Teilwertabschreibung*). The write-down is deductible for corporate income tax purposes (but not for trade tax purposes) and offsets the dividend income received.*

The corporate income tax paid by the target company on the gain realised on the sale of its assets (including the dividend withholding tax deducted from its dividend) can be recovered by NewCo. NewCo accounts for the target company's assets, including goodwill, at fair market value and starts to depreciate or amortise the acquired assets on the basis of the stepped-up book values.

The end result of this somewhat complicated structure is that, although the original acquisition takes place as a "share" deal, NewCo has all the advantages of an "asset" deal. It can use the assets and cash flow of the target to secure and service its debt and it can increase the cash

---

* The corporate income tax deductibility is excluded under s 50c of the Income Tax Act (*Einkommensteuergesetz*) where the shares in the target company were held by foreigners within the last 10 years prior to the acquistion.

flow available from tax savings generated by the step-up. The price for this benefit consists of trade tax on income (and an increased real estate transfer tax if the target owns real estate), a cost which is, however, normally more than outweighed by the substantial income tax savings. In addition, this structure may result in timing and liquidity problems and, of course, it entails all the contractual difficulties of an asset deal (see also p. 56 *et seq.* above).

(iii) Reorganisation Model

The new Act on Taxation of Reorganisations, which came into effect on 1st January 1995, has created the opportunity to carry out a step-up in a more efficient way. In cases where the target company is a corporation, its assets may be stepped up by reorganising the target into a partnership. This can be achieved without the drawbacks, in particular without incurring the trade tax cost associated with the combination model. The reorganisation model is explained in more detail on p. 123 below.

(iv) Accretion Model

This model is typically used when the target company is a GmbH & Co. KG, i.e. a limited partnership with a GmbH as the general partner. There are various possibilities for structuring the model, but the most common two work as follows:

NewCo first acquires all the interests of the limited partner in the KG and all shares in the general partner GmbH. This allows Newco to revalue the book value of the assets of the KG up to the purchase price paid for the interests of the limited partner. Thereafter, the general partner GmbH withdraws from the KG, if it has an equity interest in the partnership, in return for adequate compensation. Upon withdrawal of the general partner GmbH, all assets and liabilities of the KG are transferred by operation of law to Newco as the sole remaining partner. At the same time the KG disappears as a legal entity because there is only one partner left.

As an alternative, the investor group may first acquire only the shares in the general partner GmbH and capitalise the general partner GmbH. Thereafter, the limited partners may withdraw in return for compensation from the general partner GmbH. This also causes the partnership to disappear as a legal entity and results in the accrual of all its assets and liabilities to the remaining sole shareholder, in this case the general partner GmbH, functioning as NewCo.

It should be noted that the transaction structures outlined above have not yet been tested in the courts in the context of leveraged transactions.

Whether they will stand up against a challenge by a creditor or receiver in the case of bankruptcy remains to be seen. Moreover, they require 100% of the target to be acquired. Where this is not the case, minority rights may render these concepts impracticable.

(d) Management Duties in MBOs

The involvement of management in an MBO raises particular questions regarding the duties of management. The answers to these questions have to be derived from general principles of law. Due to the lack of applicable court decisions, there is still considerable uncertainty.

Under corporate law, the members of the management both of an AG and of a GmbH are prohibited from disclosing confidential information concerning their company to third parties. The management is, in addition, usually in a contractual relationship with the target company. The individual service agreements will expressly or impliedly provide for a number of obligations on the part of the management. As a rule, management has to render its entire working capacity to the business, it owes a fiduciary duty to the business, it is precluded from passing any confidential information to third parties and it is subject to a prohibition against competing with the business. Management may risk violating all these obligations if it prepares the buy-out without the target company's prior consent. A violation of these duties may result in civil and even criminal liabilities. Equity investors and lenders dealing with management may also run the risk of being sued for inducing a breach of contract and may even be subject to criminal liability themselves. In order to avoid these risks, management of the target company should obtain the prior consent of all shareholders of the target company as soon as possible for any preparatory measures planned in connection with an MBO.

Conflicts of interest may occur during the buy-out negotiations. Where an MBO is structured as an "asset" deal, it is theoretically conceivable that management negotiates on both sides of the table. Even if this dual function is legally permissible, it should be avoided. Good practice would normally dictate that the negotiations on the seller's side should be carried out by management members who are not part of the buy-out team, and that the negotiations on the buyer's side are left so far as possible in the hands of the other investors and external advisers.

Managing directors and members of the board of management owe a fiduciary duty not only to their company but also to its shareholders. Depending on the circumstances, they may be deemed to be under an obligation to disclose their insider information to the selling shareholders. This may in turn require disclosure of factors which could increase the value of the shares and hence the purchase price. If the directors or management board members negligently or deliberately ignore this disclosure obligation, they can become personally liable for the damages suffered by the selling shareholders. This results from the requirement of fair dealing in contractual negotiations (*culpa in contrahendo*).

VI. COMMON FINANCING METHODS

1. Introduction

Acquisitions require to be financed, whether from internal or external sources or both. The means of procuring internal financing for an acquisition are manifold. They include the generation of additional cash flow, in particular by tax savings from higher depreciation or amortisation resulting from an asset step-up, the divestment of disposable assets and sale and leaseback transactions. Internal financing methods will not be considered further at this stage. The instruments of external financing are equity and debt. Debt may be divided into senior debt and mezzanine debt. Mezzanine debt covers any hybrid form of debt ranking between senior debt and equity.

2. Equity

Equity is capital provided by the owners of the business and the company respectively. It is committed capital and, unlike a loan to the business or company, it cannot be freely withdrawn. Equity ranks last in the event of bankruptcy or liquidation. The form equity takes will depend on the type of business organisation concerned.

(a) Company with Limited Liability — GmbH

A GmbH is funded with equity primarily by payment of the share capital contributions. For each share capital contribution there is a corresponding share. The allotment of a share for a share capital contribution lower than its stated value is not permissible. However, the articles may provide that shares can be issued at a premium (*Aufgeld*) in addition to their stated nominal value. This premium is equity, but without forming part of the share capital. In the financial statements of the company it is recorded as part of the capital reserves (*Kapitalrücklagen*). At least 25% of the cash contributions to the share capital must be paid prior to the application for registration of the

GmbH. The balance as well as any premium must be paid as provided for in the articles or, if not addressed in the articles, when requested by shareholders' resolution. Special rules apply to contributions in kind and in case of a GmbH with only one shareholder.

The GmbH Act provides considerable flexibility to create and fashion many different rights and obligations for shareholders in a GmbH. Such rights and obligations may either be attached to particular shares or attached to specific shareholders personally.

The articles of association can increase the statutory rights of individual shareholders. When the increased rights attach to particular shares, such shares are usually referred to as "preferential shares" (*Vorzugsgeschäftsanteile*). When the increased rights are granted to specific shareholders personally, such rights are usually referred to as "special privileges" (*Sondervorteile*). Except for the capital preservation rules and the corporate principle of equal treatment, the freedom of the shareholders to create preferential shares and special privileges is almost unrestricted. The articles may provide, for example, for enhanced rights to the liquidation proceeds, pre-emptive rights with respect to the shares of other shareholders, increased voting rights, veto rights with respect to specified shareholders' resolutions or rights to appoint managing directors or to be appointed as managing director.

The articles of association can also increase the statutory obligations of shareholders. Such additional obligations are usually referred to as "ancillary obligations" (*Nebenleistungspflichten*). Like shareholder rights, shareholder obligations may either be attached to particular shares or bind specific shareholders personally. The creation of ancillary obligations can serve many purposes. For instance, the articles may contain an obligation to provide the company with financial resources in addition to share capital contributions, or to make specific assets available to the company or to serve as managing director of the company. Ancillary obligations will often be used to balance preferential rights or special privileges allocated to a share or shareholder.

Shareholders may not only provide equity to the company by payment of share capital contributions (including surplus) but also by payment of supplementary contributions (*Nachschüsse*). The articles of association may provide that the shareholders shall have the right to call for supplementary contributions from shareholders in proportion to their shares. Supplementary contributions are payable in addition to the share capital contribution. The obligation to make supplementary contributions, when called for, may be limited to a specified amount or unlimited. Although supplementary contributions constitute equity, they are different from share capital. Supplementary contributions can be claimed by and repaid to the shareholders more easily than share capital contributions.

(b) Stock Corporation — AG

An AG is funded with equity primarily by payment of the share capital contributions. The AG issues shares of stock. The aggregate nominal value of all outstanding shares is equal to the share capital. The issue of a share for a share capital contribution lower than its stated value is not permissible. However, the articles may provide that shares be issued for a premium (*Aufgeld*) in addition to their stated value. The premium is equity without being part of the share capital.

The shares are typically bearer shares (*Inhaberaktien*), which must be fully paid up. Registered shares (*Namensaktien*), which are relatively rare, may be issued against a minimum payment on issue of 25% of the par value plus the full amount of the premium, if any.

The basic type of shares are the ordinary or common shares (*Stammaktien*). They afford their holders the same rights (rights to dividends declared and liquidation surplus and voting rights) in proportion to the nominal value of the shares held. However, an AG may issue different classes of shares affording different rights to shareholders, in particular with regard to dividends or liquidation surplus. The ability to issue shares which impose obligations on shareholders additional to their obligation to pay up the full nominal value of the shares is limited. In particular, the law does not provide for any obligation to make supplementary contributions (*Nachschüsse*) attaching to the shares. Only such ancillary obligations (*Nebenleistungsverpflichtungen*) as represent recurring non-monetary contributions, such as services or supplies, may be attached to shares.

All classes of shares which are not common shares are collectively called preferred shares (*Vorzugsaktien*). The rights of a holder of preferred shares may be better or more restricted than those of a holder of common shares. Preferred shares may be issued as voting or as non-voting shares. Non-voting preferred shares are the customary type of preferred shares. They may only be issued with a cumulative preference as to dividends. Their aggregate par value must not exceed the aggregate par value of the voting shares. Voting preferred shares are rare and the issue of shares with multiple voting rights is generally not permissible.

It is possible to create special privileges and obligations which do not attach to particular shares but to specific shareholders personally. In particular, shareholders may personally undertake to make equity contributions to the company. In all cases where special privileges or special obligations of shareholders are created the requirement of equal treatment has to be considered. This requirement may be waived by the shareholders concerned and the Stock Corporation Act permits exceptions in some instances, e.g. for the creation of different classes of shares.

(c) Commercial Partnerships — OHG, KG

The law on commercial partnerships does not contain any specific rules on the provision of equity. Unlike a corporation, a partnership does not have a minimum or fixed share capital.

The partners enjoy almost unlimited freedom to structure their mutual rights and obligations and, in particular, to agree on the contributions to be made. As in a GmbH, the contributions may be many and various; they may consist of contributions to the equity in cash or in kind but also come in the form of services, supplies or the like. It is not necessary that a partner makes an equity contribution at all. The partnership agreement can provide for specific partners to have increased rights, e.g. with regard to voting, profit or liquidation proceeds, and can substantially exclude the rights of partners having no equity interest in the partnership.

3. Senior Debt

Senior debt ranks highest in the event of bankruptcy or liquidation. It typically takes the form of loans or straight bonds.

(a) Loans

Loans are in general provided by a bank or a syndicate of banks. The customary loan to finance an acquisition is the term loan which may be secured or unsecured. As a rule, the lender will seek security for the loan.

If real estate is available as security, a mortgage loan may be obtained from mortgage banks or savings banks or (for medium-term financing) from commercial banks. Mortgage loans generally offer better interest rates than ordinary term loans but the amount available will usually be limited to a certain percentage (50 to 60%) of the value of the real estate serving as security.

Another form of term loan is the loan against acknowledgment of receipt (*Schuldscheindarlehen*). The Schuldscheindarlehen is usually a long-term loan which comes close to a bond issue in terms of size. The loan is evidenced by a simple non-negotiable receipt (*Schuldschein*) in which the borrower acknowledges the receipt of the principal. The Schuldscheindarlehen is designed for prime borrowers only because, although the lenders are initially banks, it will eventually be placed with insurance companies, pension funds and other institutional investors. A Schuldscheindarlehen is cheaper (and certainly simpler) than a bond issue, although the associated interest rates are generally somewhat higher.

Term loans will often be supplemented by a short-term working capital facility which is typically provided on an overdraft basis. The borrower may draw on the loan from time to time to the extent required. Interest is payable only on the portion actually used; however, there may be a commitment fee on the unused balance. The interest rate is usually not fixed but subject to change upon the bank giving notice thereof.

Loans may also be provided by the owners of the borrowing company. They may choose this form of financing because they do not wish to assume the higher risks involved with an injection of equity. Moreover, when a corporation is being financed by a foreign shareholder, debt financing will often be attractive for tax reasons. This is due to the high level of German corporate income taxation. Corporations have to pay income tax at the rate of 30% on distributed profits and dividends are subject to a withholding tax of 25%, unless the withholding tax is reduced to a lower percentage by a tax treaty. Interest paid on a shareholder loan, on the other hand, constitutes a deductible business expense which reduces the corporate income tax base of the corporation and is generally not subject to taxation in Germany in the hands of a foreign shareholder. This usually makes debt financing for a foreign shareholder more advantageous than equity financing, but this financing method has been restricted by s 8a of the Corporate Income Tax Act (see pp. 103–105 below). Moreover although the owner of a company is in general free to decide whether to provide debt or equity finance, under certain circumstances debt may be re-classified and treated as equity, as will be outlined below.

(b) Straight Bonds

Straight bonds, as opposed to profit-sharing bonds, convertible bonds and option bonds, qualify as senior debt. The issue of straight bonds is legally available to all business forms. However, the credit standing required to place financing instruments of this kind successfully in the market generally means that only large AGs and (rarely) GmbHs qualify to issue straight bonds. As a rule, straight bonds of domestic industrial companies are secured by first-ranking land charges (*Grundschulden*) up to 40% of the loan value of the charged premises.

4. Mezzanine Debt

Mezzanine debt bridges the gap between equity and senior debt in an acquisition. Simply stated, mezzanine debt is any form of financing ranking ahead of equity and (at least in certain respects) behind senior debt in the event of bankruptcy or liquidation.

Mezzanine debt in Germany is rarer and less sophisticated than in other countries. Nevertheless, German law offers a variety of forms suitable for mezzanine finance, such as

- subordinated loans;
- profit-sharing loans (*partiarische Darlehen*), which are loans carrying interest dependent on the profit of the borrower;
- silent partnerships (*stille Gesellschaft*), providing for a capital contribution by the silent partner to the company and the silent partner's right to participate in the company's profits and, perhaps, losses;
- corporate profit participation certificates (*Genusscheine*), highly flexible hybrid instruments, typically evidencing the right to share in the profits (and, where the terms of issue so provide, in the liquidation surplus) of the issuer without entitlement to vote or to have an equity interest in the issuer;
- profit sharing bonds (*Gewinnschuldverschreibungen*), granting the bond holders, in addition to or in lieu of a fixed or floating rate of interest, a bonus determined on the basis of the profits realised by the issuer or another company;
- convertible bonds (*Wandelschuldverschreibungen*), granting the bondholders, in addition to interest on the principal of the bonds, the right to convert the bonds within a specified period into a certain number of shares of the issuer or another company;
- option bonds (*Optionsschuldverschreibungen*), granting the bondholders, in addition to interest on the principal of the bonds, the option to subscribe within a specified period to new shares of the issuer or another company at a price which is fixed in the terms of the issue;
- seller's notes.

The issue of bonds and corporate profit participation certificates will usually be limited to large AGs because only they have the credit standing necessary to place financing instruments of this kind successfully in the market. However, even for corporations which qualify in this respect, the issue of such instruments will usually be too difficult and time-consuming, in particular when stock exchange listing is sought, for them to be useful as a primary source of finance for an acquisition. At present, mezzanine finance for acquisitions usually takes the form of subordinated loans.

5. Capitalisation Rules

(a) Under-Capitalisation

The law provides for minimum capitalisation only for specific company forms. A GmbH, for instance, must have a minimum share capital of DM50,000, whereas the minimum share capital of an AG is DM100,000. No statutory minimum capitalisation exists for partnerships. The statutory minimum capitalisation requirements are of an abstract nature and do not ensure that any given company is sufficiently financed with equity in the light of the type and scope of its activities.

There are no general rules of law requiring that a company be adequately provided with equity. The under-capitalisation of a corporation, however, may in exceptional cases result in the personal liability of its shareholders. The corporate veil may be pierced, for example when fraudulent actions on the part of the shareholders are involved or when the business of an under-capitalised corporation has been conducted as a branch of the shareholder and goes bankrupt.

(b) Debt–Equity Ratio

There are no legal principles requiring a specific ratio between debt financing on the one hand and equity financing on the other. In general, the shareholders or partners (as the case may be) are free to choose whether to make funds available as debt or as equity. However, two restrictions have to be observed.

(1) *Equity-Replacing Loans*
A shareholder granting a loan to his company is generally treated like any other third party. He can charge interest, take security and require the repayment of the loan when due. In the event of bankruptcy or liquidation, he is on an equal footing with other third party creditors with regard to his loan. However, under certain circumstances, a shareholder loan may be considered "equity-replacing" with the consequence that it is treated as akin to equity.

A loan is defined by the GmbH Act to be equity-replacing if it is "made by a shareholder at a time when shareholders acting as orderly businessmen would instead have provided equity to the company" (s 32a, para 1). The test to be used is whether the company would have obtained the loan in question at arm's-length market terms from an unrelated third party. If the answer is in the negative, the loan is categorised as equity-replacing.

Equity-replacing loans can be provided by shareholders of a GmbH, regardless of their interest in the company. A shareholder of an AG can also grant an equity-replacing loan, provided that he holds an "entrepreneurial" interest, which is generally deemed to exist if the interest exceeds 25%. Finally, a loan given by a partner of a commercial partnership (OHG or KG) having no natural person as a general partner (GmbH & Co.) can qualify as equity-replacing as well.

The repayment of an equity-replacing loan is subject to restrictions which depend on the legal nature of the borrower and on whether the claim for repayment is made prior to or during bankruptcy or composition proceedings for the avoidance of bankruptcy.

In essence, the applicable restrictions result in a subordination of the shareholder loan making it equivalent to equity. During bankruptcy or composition proceedings of a GmbH, for example, the shareholder lender cannot require repayment of an equity-replacing loan. The loan is treated as share capital and security provided therefor by the company cannot be realised.

(2) *Thin Capitalisation Rules*
With effect from 1st January 1994 Germany has for the first time introduced statutory thin capitalisation rules. A new s 8a of the Corporate Income Tax Act limits the ability of foreign shareholders to finance their German corporate subsidiaries with debt. If the limitations of the law are not complied with, payments made by the German subsidiary to the foreign shareholder in respect of the shareholder-provided debt are not deductible as a business expense from taxable income that is subject to corporate income tax but re-characterised as profit distributions (constructive dividends). The general "dealing at arm's length" requirement applies in addition with regard to the amount of consideration paid (e.g. the rate of interest on a shareholder loan). In brief, s 8a provides for the following:

The statutory rules apply to compensations paid by a German corporation on debt provided by a shareholder which (a) is not entitled to imputation credits for corporate income tax and (b) holds a "substantial interest" in the corporation. Shareholders not entitled to imputation credits for corporate income tax are in particular foreign shareholders. A "substantial interest" is in particular given if the shareholder holds directly or indirectly an interest of more than 25% of the share capital or if the shareholder, alone or in cooperation with other shareholders, controls the corporation. The rules do not only apply in respect of debt provided by a qualifying shareholder, but also to compensations on debt provided by parties "related" to such a shareholder (e.g. foreign affiliates) or by third parties having recourse against such a shareholder or a party "related" to it (e.g. a bank in a back-to-back arrangement).

Compensations on debt are re-characterised if and to the extent that the debt provided by a shareholder exceeds the permissible limit. The permissible debt limit is determined in relation to the size of the equity interest held by such shareholder. The maximum debt-to-equity ratio depends on the nature of the debt and on whether the borrower qualifies as a holding company:

- For **ordinary loans** (in particular fixed interest loans) the debt-to-equity ratio must not exceed 9 to 1 for holding companies and 3 to 1 for other companies. These safe haven ratios can be exceeded if the borrower is able to prove that an unrelated party would have granted the loan under the same conditions and subject to the same terms.
- For all **other types of debt** (such as profit-participating loans) the debt-to-equity ratio is 0.5 to 1. This safe haven ratio cannot be exceeded, even if the borrower could prove that the loan would have also been available from an unrelated party.
- The ratios mentioned before do not apply cumulatively but concurrently. If, for instance, an ordinary loan and a profit-participating loan are combined, only such portion of the share-holders' equity which has not been used against the profit participating loan can be used to calculate the permissible amount of the ordinary loan.

Holding companies, which enjoy the special debt-to-equity ratio of 9 to 1 with regard to ordinary loans, have been defined as corporations

- whose main activity is to hold interests in and finance other corporations, or
- 75% of whose gross assets consist in interests in other corporations.

The tax administration assumes that the main activity of a corporation lies in the holding and financing of other corporations if, during the last three years, at least 75% of its gross income have been dividends and interest from subsidiaries. In order to qualify, a holding company must hold interests in at least two operative corporations and each interest should exceed 20% of the respective corporation's share capital.

Two additional rules are particularly important. First, for purposes of calculating the applicable ratios, the equity of a non-holding company is reduced by the book value of its interest in a subsidiary. Second, no safe haven ratio applies to foreign shareholder debt provided directly to a subsidiary of a holding company (i.e. re-characterisation can only be avoided in case of ordinary loan if the subsidiary can prove availability of loan from unrelated sources). Therefore, a foreign shareholder should, in general, lend to a German holding company (not to a subsidiary of a holding company) and to subsidiaries of non-holding companies (not to non-holding companies themselves).

6. Financial Assistance

When debt finance is being used to finance an acquisition, the repayment of both capital and interest often have to be borne by the acquired business. Moreover, senior lenders will regularly, and mezzanine lenders will occasionally, require that the acquired business serve as security for the finance.

In the case of an asset purchase transaction, the fulfilment of these requirements provides no serious difficulty. The business acquired can be used to service the debt. Accounts receivable can be assigned for security purposes (*Sicherungsabtretung*), title to moveable assets and inventory can be transferred as security (*Sicherungsübereignung*) and real estate and buildings can also be charged (*Grundpfandrechte*).

In the case of a share purchase transaction matters are more difficult. It is, of course, possible to pledge the shares in the target company to the lenders as security. However, this is not satisfactory from the financiers' point of view because a pledge over the shares ranks behind the creditors of the target. The provision of financial assistance by the target company itself, however, is basically prohibited by the capital preservation rules of German law. The capital preservation rules applying when shares or interests in a company are acquired will vary according to the legal form of the target. These rules, as well as the structures designed to overcome the problems stemming therefrom, are discussed in the context of leveraged transactions on p. 91 *et seq.* above.

7. Securities Law

(a) No Requirement of Governmental Approval

Neither the issue of equity securities nor the issue of debt securities requires any governmental approval. The former approval requirement for certain debt instruments, in particular bearer bonds issued within Germany, has been abolished as from 1st January 1991.

The Securities Prospectus Act (*Wertpapier-Verkaufsprospektgestz*) which came into force on 1st January 1991 requires, as a rule, that a prospectus be published for all securities which are offered to the public for the first time in Germany and which are not admitted to trading on a German stock exchange (s 1). Numerous exemptions from this disclosure requirement exist, depending on the type of offer, security and issuer concerned. For instance, debt securities issued by a German credit institution which routinely offers debt securities to the public, and all Euro-bonds which are not subject to public promotion, are exempted (s 3, No. 2 and s 4, para 1, No. 1). The prospectus must contain, generally speaking, all information which is necessary to enable the public to make a proper assessment of the issuer and the securities being offered (ss 5 and 7). As a rule, the prospectus will not be approved or even examined by any authority. Only when an admission to the official market of a German stock exchange has been applied for with regard to the securities concerned, will the approval of the prospectus by the admission office (*Zulassungsstelle*) of the stock exchange be necessary. The obligation to issue a prospectus is supplemented by a rigorous liability of the issuer for incorrect, incomplete or misleading statements in the prospectus.

(b) Regulatory Authority and Stock Exchange

In the past, there was no German domestic authority responsible for enforcing the statutory provisions for the issuance and trading of securities, comparable, e.g., to the SEC in the US. This situation has changed radically, though, as from 1st January 1995. In an effort to improve the attractiveness and international competitiveness of Germany as a financial market, the Securities Trading Act (*Wertpapierhandelsgesetz*) has been passed which introduces for the first time a federal supervisory authority overseeing certain aspects of the issuance and trading of securities (*Bundesaufsichtsamt für den Wertpapierhandel*). The responsibilities of the new authority comprise in particular the following:

- control of compliance with the new insider rules (see pp. 43–44 above);
- control of ad hoc disclosure by companies listing securities (see pp. 31–32 above);
- control of the new disclosure rules regarding transactions involving major holdings in listed companies (see pp. 32–35 above);
- cooperation with foreign supervisory authorities and international organisations.

Within its scope of authority, the Bundesaufsichtsamt may issue and enforce orders and impose penalties of up to DM50,000 and administrative fines of up to DM3,000,000. Illegal insider trading will qualify as a crime and, as such, be subject to prosecution by the competent district attorney's office.

There are eight stock exchanges in Germany, the most important being those in Frankfurt am Main and Düsseldorf. The stock exchanges are organised pursuant to the Stock Exchange Act (*Börsengesetz*). They are subject to the supervision of their respective state governments. The Second Act on the Promotion of Financial Markets of July 1994 has significantly intensified the level of control over the stock exchanges. In particular, each stock exchange will have to establish a trading supervisory board (*Handelsüberwachungsstelle*) which shall control the trading activities in the respective stock exchange and report to the competent state supervisory authority. Each stock exchange has its own rules on the admission and trading of securities.

The stock exchange market falls into three segments, namely,

* the official market (*Amtlicher Handel*),
* the regulated market (*Geregelter Markt*) and
* the semi-official market (*Freiverkehr*).

The admission of securities to trading on a stock exchange is regulated by the Stock Exchange Act and the rules of the individual stock exchanges. The admission to the official and regulated market is made on the basis of a prospectus and, in the case of admission to the official market, must be sponsored by a bank which is admitted to the relevant stock exchange. The listing procedure depends on the market segment to which admission is sought. Bonds must be in bearer form in order to qualify for stock exchange listing. Once securities have been listed, the issuer is subject to broad disclosure obligations, in particular with regard to facts which might influence the value of the securities (see pp. 31–32 above).

8. Availability of Local Financing

There are a large number of different types of financial institutions in Germany providing both debt and equity.

Banks generally operate as so-called universal banks (*Universalbanken*). The universal banks fall into three categories: the commercial banks (*private Geschäftsbanken*) organised under private law, the savings banks (*Sparkassen*) and their central banks (*Landesbanken-Girozentralen*) organised under public law and the credit associations (*Kreditgenossenschaften*) organised under the law of cooperatives. The universal banks provide a full range of banking, financial and investment banking services.

Commercial banks are very much engaged in the short and medium-term lending business, invest in securities for their own account, deal in securities for their customers, act as proxies for their customers who have deposited their stock with them and quite often hold substantial equity interests in many industries. There are more than 300 commercial banks. The three leading commercial banks are Deutsche Bank AG, Dresdner Bank AG and Commerzbank AG.

The savings banks, as their name implies, focus on the acceptance of savings deposits. As lenders, they engage primarily in real estate lending business. Although they have very much expanded their activities into the area of commercial banking, they are still subject to a number of restrictions. Apart from the almost 700 local savings banks there are 13 regional institutions (*Landesbanken-Girozentralen*) and a central institution (*Deutsche Girozentrale-Deutsche Kommunalbank*) which act as central banks and clearing houses for the local savings banks but also engage in substantial banking activities on their own account.

The credit associations originally provided their services only to their members, primarily farmers, craftsmen and small businesses. They now aim at a broader clientele but still focus on the savings and short and medium-term lending business. There are more than 2500 credit associations. Their central institution is the DG Bank Deutsche Genossenschaftsbank.

Some banking institutions have limited their activities to particular services. These specialised banks comprise in particular mortgage banks (*Hypothekenbanken*) and special purpose banks (*Kreditinstitute mit Sonderaufgaben*), such as Industrie-Kreditbank AG — Deutsche Industriebank which primarily extends medium and long-term credits to small and medium-sized firms or Kreditanstalt für Wiederaufban (KfW) which finances exports to developing countries but also domestic investments in economically disadvantaged and structurally weak regions.

Whereas the banks will typically function as providers of debt, equity may be obtained from a considerable number of capital investment companies (*Kapitalbeteiligungsgesellschaften*), venture capital companies and specialised LBO/MBO funds.

Capital investment companies aim to acquire minority interests in profitable, well-managed medium-sized companies, in order to place these interests at some later date with the public. It is estimated that there are some 100 companies of this type but, generally speaking, their performance has not yet proved satisfactory.

Venture capital companies aim to finance young and innovative businesses with growth potential and may often provide their own management for the venture. Although the operating philosophies of capital investment companies and of venture capital companies are different in theory, the actual business policies of each type of company have in practice become increasingly similar. In particular, venture capital companies have become more active in the MBO market, although the acquisition of well-established businesses is not the classical approach for venture capital investments.

As from 1st January 1987, a new type of investment company has been introduced, the so-called *Unternehmensbeteiligungsgesellschaft*. This investment company is designed to collect investment funds for equity contributions to non-listed medium-sized companies. The Unternehmensbeteiligungsgesellschaft must be established in the legal form of an AG, its minimum share capital must be DM2m and its shareholders must undertake to offer within 10 years at least 70% of all shareholdings to the public through the stock exchanges. The investment activities of the Unternehmensbeteiligungsgesellschaft are severely restricted. Due to these restrictions and the full taxation of capital gains realised by the company in the event of divestment, the Unternehmensbeteiligungsgesellschaft has not proved very popular.

VII. TAXATION ASPECTS

As is usual in all industrial countries, the German tax system is complex. There are many different taxes imposed on a federal, state and, to a limited extent, even a municipal level. The following outline is intended to address some basic aspects of German taxation relevant to acquisitions and mergers.

1. Principles of Tax System and Relevant Taxes

(a) Individual Income Tax (*Einkommensteuer*)

Individual income tax is imposed on resident and non-resident individuals. The tax base for residents is their worldwide net income.

Non-residents are subject to income tax only with regard to specific German-source income which is explicitly defined in the relevant statute (Income Tax Act, s 49).

The general tax rate starts at 25.9% with a straight line progression up to a top tax bracket of 53% (Income Tax Act, s 32a). The top tax bracket applies to an annual net income exceeding DM120,041. The general tax rate is subject to various exceptions. A special reduced marginal tax rate of 47% applies to individual income from trade or business (*gewerbliche Einkünfte*) (s 32c). This reduced rate is meant to counterbalance the trade tax levied on income from trade or business.

(b) Corporate Income Tax (*Körperschaftsteuer*)

A resident corporation, i.e. a corporation having either its statutory seat or place of management and control in Germany, is generally subject to corporate income tax on its worldwide net income. Tax treaties may exempt certain types of foreign income from German taxation.

Germany has a split corporate income tax system. The tax rate differs depending on whether profits are retained in the company or distributed to the shareholders. The tax rate on retained profits is 45% (Corporate Income Tax Act, s 23). Profits distributed are subject to a tax rate of 30% (Corporate Income Tax Act, s 27). In addition, there is a 25% dividend withholding tax. The rate of the dividend withholding tax levied on profits distributed to foreign shareholders may be reduced under a tax treaty. Most German tax treaties provide for a reduction to 15%. In the future, the rate will in many cases decrease to only 5%. Following Article 10 of the OECD Model Convention, the modern German tax treaties tend to provide for a reduction to 5% for intercorporate share holdings (*Schachtelbeteiligungen*) and 15% for portfolio investments (*Streubesitz*). Under the US–German tax treaty for instance, the withholding tax has been reduced in general to 5% where the shareholder holds directly at least 10% of the voting shares of the corporation and to 10% in all other cases. No dividend withholding tax is charged on profits distributed after 30 June 1996 to parent corporations which hold at least a 25% capital interest and are domiciled in an EU country (Income Tax Act, s 44d).

The corporate income tax system is an imputation system. If the pre-tax profits are DM100 and if, after deduction of the corporate income tax of DM30, a cash dividend of DM70 is distributed, a German shareholder would report a dividend income of DM100 and claim an imputation credit of DM30 (or 3/7 of the cash dividend of DM70) against his (individual income or corporate income) tax liability. The same would apply with regard to the dividend withholding tax of DM17.5 (= 25% of the cash dividend of DM70). In other words, the corporate income tax liability and the withholding tax paid by the corporation can be fully credited against the individual income or corporate income tax of its shareholder. Both types of credit are refundable tax credits. Consequently dividend income will ultimately be taxed only at the rate applicable to the recipient.

Non-resident shareholders, whether individuals or companies, do not qualify for the imputation system, unless the dividends paid are attributable to a German permanent establishment or fixed base. Therefore, non-resident shareholders are generally not entitled to a credit for corporate income tax and withholding tax paid by their German corporation. This results in a considerable tax burden for foreign shareholders and for this reason many foreign shareholders finance their German corporations largely by shareholder loans because interest paid thereon is a deductible business expense for corporate income tax purposes and the interest income is not taxable in Germany. As from 1994, however, the legislature has imposed statutory restrictions on this financing technique (see p. 103 *et seq.* above).

Non-resident corporations, like non-resident individuals, are subject to German corporate income tax only in relation to specific items of German-source income. The most frequently encountered type of German-source income is income generated through the operation of a permanent establishment in Germany. A permanent establishment is typically created by the operation of a branch or by the acquisition of an interest in a commercial partnership. The tax rate for non-resident corporations is in general 42%, whether or not the income is distributed by the branch to the head office or by the partnership to its partners.

A partnership is neither subject to corporate income tax nor to individual income tax. For income tax purposes it is transparent and its profits and losses are directly attributed to the partners. Profits are taxed exclusively at the partner level and subject to the individual income tax rate applicable to the individual partner. This is true whether profits are withdrawn or retained.

(c) **Solidarity Surcharge** (*Solidaritätszuschlag*)

In order to finance the costs of the German reunification, from 1995 onwards a temporary solidarity surcharge of 7.5% is levied on the total amount of the income tax or corporate income tax bill (Solidarity

Surcharge Act (*Solidaritätszuschlaggesetz*) of 23rd June 1993). A simplified imputation system applies to residents so that dividend income is only taxed once. For non-residents, however, the solidarity surcharge levied both on the corporate income tax and the dividend withholding tax is a final cost. Only where a tax treaty reduces the applicable withholding tax, no solidarity surcharge may be imposed on the withholding tax. Although temporary in nature, it is unclear when the solidarity surcharge will be abolished or reduced.

(d) Trade Tax (*Gewerbesteuer*)

Trade tax is a municipal tax which falls into two categories, namely, trade tax on income (*Gewerbeertragsteuer*) and trade tax on capital (*Gewerbekapitalsteuer*). It is imposed on most commercial or industrial activities carried out in Germany, regardless of their legal form. Partnerships are taxable entities in their own right for trade tax purposes, provided they are engaged, or deemed engaged, in commercial or industrial activities.

The trade tax on income is calculated on the basis of the income subject to individual or corporate income tax, with certain additions and deductions. For instance, 50% of interest expenses on long-term debt is not deductible as a business expense for the purposes of trade tax on income.

The trade tax on capital is based on the net equity as determined for net assets tax purposes, again adjusted by certain additions and deductions. For example, 50% of the principal in respect of long-term debt will be added back in order to establish the tax base for trade tax on capital.

Trade tax is treated as a deductible business expense for individual and corporate income tax purposes, but also for trade tax purposes. The trade tax rates are fixed by the local municipalities and vary accordingly. The effective tax rates range, in the case of trade tax on income, between 13 and 20.5% and, in the case of trade tax on capital, between 0.6 and 1.03%.

The political justification of the trade tax is highly disputed. It is suggested that the trade tax on capital, in particular, should be abolished. No trade tax on capital has been levied on businesses in Eastern Germany until the end of 1996, but it is not even clear whether this exception will be continued any longer.

(e) Net Assets Tax (*Vermögensteuer*)

The net assets tax imposed on the value of the net assets of individuals and corporations as at the beginning of each calendar year has been declared unconstitutional by the Federal Constitutional Court and is no longer levied as from 1st January 1997.*

(f) Value Added Tax (*Umsatzsteuer*)

Value added tax is payable on most business transactions effected within Germany by a so-called "entrepreneur" (*Unternehmer*), which may in general be any person engaged in business or trade in order to generate income (not necessarily profit). Individuals, corporations and partnerships, whether domestic or foreign, may be liable to pay the tax.

Transactions subject to value added tax comprise in particular the supply of goods and services. A substantial number of transactions are either not subject to tax, tax-exempt or zero-rated. For example, the transfer of shares and interests in companies is tax-exempt. The transfer of an entire business or a stand-alone business division to another entrepreneur (asset deal) is not subject to tax. The transfer of bonds and transactions covered by the Real Estate Transfer Tax Act (*Grunderwerbsteuergesetz*) are tax-exempt.

Value added tax charged by one entrepreneur to another may generally be reclaimed by the latter as input-VAT. Thus, value added tax does not constitute a final tax burden for the parties. Private consumers are not entitled to credits for value added tax charged to them and, therefore, it is they in the end who actually bear the value added tax.

The tax rate is generally 15%. However, certain goods and services are subject to a 7% rate.

(g) Capital Investment Tax (*Gesellschaftsteuer*)

The capital investment tax levied on capital contributions in cash or in kind to a German corporation or to a German limited partnership whose sole general partner is a corporation (e.g. a GmbH & Co. KG) has been abolished as from 1st January 1992.

---

*Federal Constitutional Court, decision of 22nd June 1995, DB 1995, 1740.

(h) Stock Exchange Tax (*Börsenumsatzsteuer*)

The stock exchange tax levied on the sale of shares in corporations and certain securities and similar instruments has been abolished as from 1st January 1991.

(i) Real Estate Transfer Tax (*Grunderwerbsteuer*)

The real estate transfer tax is imposed on a number of transactions involving real estate located in Germany. In particular, this tax is levied on the sale or transfer of title to real estate and on the direct or indirect acquisition of 100% of the shares in a company owning real estate by one person or a group of related persons.

The tax rate is 3.5%, the basis usually being the consideration paid for the real estate acquired. However, if the tax is triggered by the acquisition of all of the shares in a company owning real estate, the tax is calculated on the basis of the assessed tax value of such real estate, which is currently still lower than the market value.

(j) Stamp Duties and Notarial Fees

No stamp duties are payable in connection with mergers and acquisitions.

Various transactions must be recorded by a notary public in order to be effective. This is true, for example, for the sale and transfer of shares in a GmbH or of real estate. The fees of German notaries public are set by statute and depend on the value of the transaction. A transaction value of, for example, DM100m, will result in notarial fees of DM103,000. The fees for a transaction value of DM500m are DM127,000. Whether, and to what extent, notarisation by foreign notaries is sufficient for purposes of German law is still under dispute (see p. 145 *et seq.* below).

(k) Group Taxation (*Organschaft*)

The concept of group taxation affords the possibility of pooling the profits and losses of two or more legally independent taxpayers for purposes of corporate income and trade tax.

Group taxation may be established between one or more subsidiaries (*Organgesellschaft*) and their parent (*Organträger*). It requires the fulfilment of certain conditions, in particular

- the subsidiaries must be resident corporations and the parent, which may be an individual, a corporation or a partnership, must also be a German resident or a German branch (permanent

establishment) engaged in commercial or industrial activities;
- the subsidiaries must be financially, economically and organ-isationally integrated into the parent;
- for the purposes of corporate income tax *Organschaft* the sub-sidiaries and the parent company must enter into a profit and loss pooling agreement for a period of at least five years under which the subsidiaries undertake to transfer all their profits to the parent, while the parent promises to make good any losses which the subsidiaries might incur during the term of the agreement;
- the parent must have genuine economic substance. If the parent is a holding company, it must own shares in at least two companies and must act as a true management holding business.

Group taxation offers particular advantages in cases where one sub-sidiary is making losses and the parent or another subsidiary is profitable. In such cases losses and profits may be offset. However, to consolidate the profits of a subsidiary with the losses of a parent the group taxation concept is not necessary for corporate income tax purposes because the profits can be distributed to the parent and offset against its losses, which gives rise to a corporate tax refund to the parent under the imputation system. For trade tax purposes, a set-off can only be achieved through *Organschaft*.

(1) **Loss Carry-Forward** (*Verlustvortrag*) and **Loss Carry-Back** (*Verlustrücktrag*)

For personal and corporate income tax purposes a loss incurred in any fiscal year can be carried back to the two preceding years up to an aggregate amount of DM10m. Any remaining loss is carried forward for an indefinite period of time. The taxpayer is entitled to waive the carry-back in total or in part and opt for the loss carry-forward instead (Income Tax Act, s 10d and Corporate Income Tax Act, s 8, para 1).

For trade tax on income purposes, no loss carry-back is possible. However, losses are carried forward indefinitely (Trade Tax Act, s 10a).

(m) **Loss Corporations**

A tax loss and the right to the loss carry-forward are not transferable as such. This rule was often circumvented by the sale of corporate shells which had substantial tax losses. The Tax Reform Act 1990 has effectively barred this practice by providing that losses will only qualify for an offset against future profits if the corporation which incurred the losses and the corporation which makes the profits are identical both from a legal and economic point of view. Economic identity is deemed to be lacking in particular in circumstances where more than

75% of the shares have been transferred and the corporation thereafter resumes its business activities with substantially new assets (Corporate Income Tax Act, s 8, para 4 and Trade Tax Act, s 10a, sentence 4).

2. Acquisition Strategies

(a) General

Germany is a high tax jurisdiction. Naturally, both the seller and the purchaser will seek to reduce their tax burden as much as possible. The seller will try to arrange for any capital gain realised from the sale to be received free of tax, or at least at a favourable tax rate, or to roll it over. The purchaser will aim at a step-up in the tax basis of the target's assets in order to achieve higher depreciation and amortisation. Furthermore, he will try to obtain a tax deduction for the cost of his acquisition finance and to minimise transfer taxes.

The tax planning opportunities available to achieve these goals, or at least some of them, will vary depending on whether the seller is an individual or a corporation.

The two basic legal methods of acquiring a business — the share purchase transaction on the one hand and the asset purchase transaction on the other hand — entail substantially different tax consequences, both for the seller and the buyer. The sale of interests in a partnership is, in spite of its general qualification as a share transaction, treated as an asset purchase transaction for tax purposes.

(b) Share Purchase Transaction

Only the acquisition of shares in a corporation constitutes a share purchase transaction for the purposes of tax law. The acquisition of an interest in a partnership is treated like an asset purchase transaction for tax purposes.

(1) *Seller's Position*

The tax position of the seller will depend on whether the shares constitute private assets (*Privatvermögen*) or business assets (*Betriebsvermögen*). Shares owned by an individual may constitute private or business assets but shares owned by a company are always business assets. In many cases the sale of shares will be tax free or taxed at a reduced rate. This is why the share purchase transaction is often the seller's obvious choice.

(i) Shares as Private Assets

Capital gains derived from the sale of shares constituting private assets of the seller are, as a rule, tax free. There are three important exceptions to this principle:

First, if an individual resident or non-resident has held more than 25% of the shares in the target corporation at any time during the last five years, this holding is classified as a so-called "substantial participation" (*wesentliche Beteiligung*). Capital gains realised from the sale of a substantial participation are subject to personal income tax (but not to trade tax on income) (Income Tax Act, s 17). However, a reduced income tax rate of 50% of the applicable regular rate (i.e. a maximum tax rate of 26.5%) is levied on capital gains not exceeding DM30m. Capital gains in excess of DM30m will be subject to the regular tax rate (s 34). In many cases, the capital gains of non-residents will, however, be exempt from taxation in Germany by a tax treaty.

Second, if shares are sold which have not been held by the resident seller for more than six months after their acquisition, this will be deemed a speculative transaction (*Spekulationsgeschäft*), regardless of the percentage of the shares held (Income Tax Act, s 23). Capital gains resulting from such a speculative transaction are subject to personal income tax at the regular rate. This is true even if a substantial participation is being sold which would normally warrant the application of a reduced tax rate (s 23, para 3, sentence 2). In the case of a non-resident seller, only the sale of a substantial participation will give rise to treatment as a speculative transaction.

Third, any capital gains of a resident resulting from a sale of shares in a corporation which were issued as compensation for the contribution of a business or partnership (interest) to such corporation under circumstances where such corporation recorded the business or partnership (interest) so contributed below its respective fair market value (*einbringungsgeborene Anteile*) are taxable (Act on Taxation of Reorganisations, s 21, para 1). Capital gains not exceeding DM30m are taxable at a reduced rate of 50% of the applicable regular rate. Any excess capital gains are subject to the regular tax rate.

(ii) Shares as Business Assets

Capital gains derived from the sale of shares constituting business assets of the seller are, in general, subject to trade tax and taxable at full individual income or corporate income tax rates. Even the capital gains of non-resident individuals and corporations may be subject to German taxation, unless different provision has been made in an applicable tax treaty (which is in fact typically the case). Three exceptions apply to this rule:

First, taxation may be fully avoided in the case of an exchange of shares if the seller obtains as consideration shares in a different corporation which are, with regard to their value, form and function, comparable to the shares sold (Exchange opinion (*Tauschgutachten*) of the Federal Tax Court of 16th December 1958 (BStBL III 1959, 30)).

Secondly, up to 50% of the capital gains may be rolled over and remain tax free if the seller reinvests in certain assets, such as personal property or real estate. Re-investment in shares of a different corporation gives rise to rollover treatment only under very limited circumstances (Income Tax Act, s 6b).

Thirdly, if an individual seller holds and sells 100% of the shares, the capital gains up to DM30m are subject to a reduced individual income tax rate of 50% of the applicable regular rate, while only the excess amount is subject to the regular rate (Income Tax Act, s 16, para 1, No. 1 and s 34). If the seller winds up his business activities entirely, no trade tax will be levied.

(2) *Purchaser's Position*
The tax position of a purchaser of shares is, as a rule, rather disadvantageous. The acquisition cost of the shares cannot be utilised for tax purposes. Shares cannot be depreciated or amortised and the book value of the assets of the target company cannot be stepped up. Thus, a share purchase transaction will not result in the increased depreciation or amortisation and improved cash flow which the purchaser might require to service the acquisition financing. Only in exceptional cases can the purchaser write down the shares if they belong to his business assets and their market value following acquisition falls below their book value. A loss carry-forward will be preserved by a share transaction.

Financing costs for the acquisition may generally be deducted from German taxable income. However, a direct acquisition of shares in a German target company by a foreign company would, as a rule, not be sufficient to achieve a deduction of borrowing costs. Most of the tax treaties into which Germany has entered with other countries follow the OECD Model Convention and exempt substantial foreign holdings in a German corporation from German taxation. This affords the foreign shareholder protection against German taxation in the event of a disposal of its interest but, on the other hand, prevents the deductibility of financing costs in Germany.

In order to achieve a tax deduction for his financing costs in Germany, the foreign purchaser will usually interpose a German resident corporation which will acquire the shares of the target company and take up the necessary acquisition borrowings, including shareholder loans. It should be noted that the interposition of a German corporation creates the disadvantage that any capital gain derived from a subsequent sale of shares in the target company will be subject to German taxation. This disadvantage can be avoided, however, if shares in the holding company rather than shares in the target company are sold, provided that the shareholder of the holding company has protection under the applicable tax treaty.

Interposing a German resident corporation as acquisition vehicle can achieve additional benefits if such corporation qualifies as a holding company. A holding company is entitled to a favourable debt–equity ratio under the thin capitalisation rules so that shareholder financing should be channelled through a holding company (see pp. 103–105 above). In addition, a holding company would allow group taxation to be established between the holding and its subsidiaries (see pp. 114–115 above).

(c) **Asset Purchase Transaction**

For purposes of tax law, not only the acquisition of individual assets but also the acquisition of interests in a partnership will constitute an asset purchase transaction.

(1) Seller's Position
If a corporation sells assets, capital gains derived therefrom are part of its ordinary income and, therefore, subject to corporate income tax and trade tax at ordinary rates. Limited exceptions may apply if and to the extent that the requirements for reinvestment in accordance with s 6(b) of the Income Tax Act can be fulfilled. Tax is levied whether the seller is a resident corporation or a non-resident corporation disposing of assets of a permanent establishment in Germany. For a German-resident corporate seller, therefore, it is taxwise in general irrelevant whether shares or assets are being sold.

If a partnership or a sole proprietor sells assets, capital gains derived therefrom are generally subject to personal income and trade tax. However, capital gains are trade tax free and gains of up to DM30m are subject to a reduced personal income tax rate of 50% of the regular income tax if the assets sold constitute the entire business or a division (*Teilbetrieb*) of the partnership or sole proprietorship (Income Tax Act, s 16, para 1, No. 1 and s 34). The reduced rate is not available insofar as the same persons participate both on the seller side and on the buyer side (owner buy-out) (s 16, para 2, sentence 3). Corporate partners of a partnership, however, have in any case to pay corporate income tax at its ordinary rate and not at a privileged rate.

If an interest in a partnership is sold, any capital gains of individual partners up to DM30m are taxed at half the normal rate (50% of up to 53%) and trade tax on income can be avoided under normal circumstances (s 16, para 1, No. 2 and s 34). Again, the reduced rate is not available insofar as the same persons participate both on the seller side and the buyer side. Corporate partners, on the other hand, pay the full corporate tax rate (45% for resident corporations and 42% for non-resident corporations) but are exempt from trade tax if they dispose of an interest in a partnership (see Trade Tax Regulations, s 40(2)).

(2) *Purchaser's Position*

The purchaser of assets has a very favourable tax position. The acquisition costs can be directly allocated to the various assets acquired. This will usually allow the purchaser to step up the tax basis of the acquired assets. Depreciation and amortisation can then be taken from the stepped-up basis, thus reducing the taxable income and increasing the cash flow of the purchaser.

The allocation of the acquisition costs has to be effected in four consecutive steps as follows:

- First, the costs have to be allocated to the capitalised assets up to their market value.
- Secondly, the costs have to be allocated to individual, intangible assets (e.g. trade marks, patents, know-how, software) which have not yet been capitalised.
- Thirdly, any remaining acquisition costs constitute goodwill which has to be amortised over 15 years (Income Tax Act, s 7, para 1, sentence 3).
- Fourthly, insofar as an allocation cannot be made under the first three steps, the costs in question may, in rather exceptional cases, be immediately deducted as a business expense.

The purchaser of an interest in a partnership is treated as if he had purchased assets, because a partnership is transparent for income tax purposes. The difference between the acquisition cost and the nominal amount of the capital account of the seller is allocated in accordance with the procedure referred to above, then capitalised and written down in a so-called supplementary balance sheet (*Ergänzungsbilanz*).

The purchaser of assets will normally establish a German acquisition company which takes up the necessary financing and which can deduct the interest paid thereon from its income. For the acquisition of a partnership interest it is not necessary to interpose a German acquiring company, even if the purchaser is a non-resident. Any interest paid by a resident or non-resident partner for the acquisition financing of his participation will qualify as a business expense and reduce his taxable partnership income. However, because of the applicable corporate income tax rate of 42% where a non-resident corporation holds an interest in a German partnership, a non-resident buyer will generally be interested in holding the partnership interest through a German-resident corporation.

Although the acquisition of a partnership interest is usually favourable both for the seller and the purchaser (because the individual seller enjoys a reduced tax rate on capital gains, while the purchaser obtains a step-up in the tax basis of the underlying assets) this structure may involve disadvantages for the purchaser. A loss carry-forward of the partnership will be lost. In the event of a subsequent disposal of his partnership interest, any capital gains derived therefrom will be subject to German taxation, whether the partner is resident or non-resident. By contrast, the disposal of a share in a corporation may be tax free in Germany, in particular if the seller is a non-resident enjoying protection under a tax treaty. A solution to this problem for a foreigner may be to interpose a corporation to acquire the partnership interest, rather than acquire the interest directly, and to sell the shares in the corporation at a later date.

(d) Combined Share and Asset Purchase Transaction

The foregoing illustrates that the acquisition of a corporation often creates a conflict of interest between the seller and the purchaser. If the owner of the corporation is an individual, the sale of shares will often be tax free or at least taxable at half the normal rate, whereas the sale of assets will be taxed at full rates. If the owner is foreign, capital gains from the sale of shares will typically be exempt from German taxation under a tax treaty, whereas the sale of assets will be subject to full taxation in Germany. In such circumstances the seller will obviously opt for a share transaction. The purchaser, however, will usually favour an asset transaction because this will allow him to step up the acquired assets and gain a higher level of depreciation or amortisation.

This conflict of interest may be resolved by an acquisition strategy which involves a combined share–asset transaction. The idea behind this model is to acquire shares and to transform the share transaction within the sphere of the purchaser into an asset transaction. This so-called "internal asset deal" may take place via the following steps:

- a German holding company is established;
- the holding company acquires the shares in the target corporation;
- thereafter, the holding company purchases, by means of an asset deal, the assets and liabilities of the target corporation at their fair market value, which is equivalent to the price paid for the shares. The target will thus realise a taxable gain. The gain is subject to corporate income tax and trade tax on income;
- the profit realised by the target corporation, including any reserves, is then distributed as dividend to the holding company;
- the holding company then writes down the value of its investment in the target corporation in an amount equal to the dividend distribution (*ausschüttungsbedingte Teilwertabschreibung*). The write-down is deductible for corporate income tax purposes (not for trade tax purposes: Trade Tax Act, s 8, No. 10a and Federal Tax Court of 2nd February 1994, DB 1994, 862), unless the shares in the target corporation were held by foreigners prior to the acquisition (Income Tax Act, s 50c). This deduction offsets the dividend income received. The corporate income tax paid by the target corporation on the gain realised on the sale of its assets (including the dividend withholding tax deducted from its dividend) can be recovered by the holding company;
- the holding company accounts for the assets acquired from the target corporation at their fair market value and starts depreciating or amortising them on the basis of the stepped-up values;
- the target corporation is left with assets equivalent to its issued share capital. It may be liquidated or used for other purposes.

The result of all this is that the seller has the benefits of a share transaction, whereas the holding company has all the advantages of an asset deal. As mentioned before, this model works only where the shares in the target corporation have not been held within the past ten years by a shareholder not resident in Germany. The price the purchaser has to pay is the cost of trade tax on income (and increased real estate transfer tax if the target corporation owns real estate) which, however, is usually more than outweighed by the tax savings gained through higher depreciation or amortisation. The combined share–asset transaction is a rather complicated acquisition method. It may be considered abusive if it lacks economic substance and is done only for tax reasons. Accordingly, it must be carefully prepared, documented and consummated in order to be successful and to withstand any challenges in the tax courts.

(e) Share Purchase Transaction with Reorganisation (Reorganisation Model)

The new Act on Taxation of Reorganisations, which came into effect on 1st January 1995, has brought about a new technique to optimise a share transaction. In cases where the target company is a corporation, its assets may be stepped up by reorganising the target into a partnership (s 3 *et seq.*). This can be achieved without the drawbacks, in particular without incurring the trade tax cost associated with the combined share and asset purchase transaction as follows:

- a German holding company and a German sister company are established;
- the holding company acquires the shares in the target corporation;
- the holding company sells a small interest in the target corporation to its sister company so that the target corporation has two shareholders;
- the target corporation thereupon reorganises as a partnership. Typically, the partnership would be a limited partnership with the holding company as limited partner and the sister company as general partner, having no equity interest in the partnership. For tax purposes, this reorganisation is treated like a merger between a corporation and a partnership and the shares of the corporation are deemed to be contributed to the partnership at acquisition cost. All assets of the target corporation pass to the partnership at their book value. No transfer gain is realised by the target corporation;
- the partnership records the assets of the target corporation at book value in its own balance sheet and replaces thereby the acquisition cost for the shares of the extinguished target corporation. This results in a "takeover loss" equal to the book value of the target corporation's assets, minus the book value of the target corporation's shares (i.e. acquisition cost), plus the amount of corporate income tax underlying the target corporation's retained earnings;
- thereupon, the partnership steps up the tax basis of the assets by the amount of the takeover loss, but not beyond fair market value;
- the partners of the partnership (i.e. the holding company and its sister company) are granted a tax credit for the corporate income tax underlying the target corporation's retained earnings.

In the end result, the reorganisation allows non-depreciable shares to be replaced by stepped-up depreciable or amortisable assets. This can be achieved without triggering any corporate income tax or trade tax on income. Like the combined share and asset purchase transaction, however, the reorganisation concept may result in increased real estate transfer tax and requires that the shares in the target corporation were not acquired from non-residents within the last ten years. A loss carry-forward of the target corporation cannot be transferred to the partnership.

3. Germany as a Location for Holding Companies

German tax law now offers a number of important benefits to the foreign corporate investor which facilitate the acquisition of German targets and can substantially reduce the tax burden on an investment in an environment otherwise known for its high location costs. Key features include the complete elimination of capital transfer taxes and stamp duties, manageable thin capitalisation rules that provide for special benefits for holding companies but remain inapplicable to partnerships, the availability of a tax-free basis step-up upon reorganisation of a German target corporation into a partnership, a complex but practicable group taxation regime, and the carry-over of losses upon mergers between corporations.

The investor will find, in addition, that German law and its extensive network of tax treaties provide a beneficial environment for the holding and operation of integrated groups of enterprises out of Germany. Key elements in regard to trans-border holdings include the following:

- the complete elimination of withholding tax on dividends paid by a German-resident corporation to EU parents (Income Tax Act, s 44d);
- the general applicability of the exemption system to intercompany dividends received by a German-resident corporation from qualifying subsidiaries that are resident in a treaty country, with the consequence that such dividends do not constitute taxable income for the recipient;
- the extension of the participation exemption to capital gains so that the disposal by a German corporation of shares held in a foreign subsidiary will no longer give rise to German tax, provided that, for instance, dividends paid on these shares would be exempt under the applicable tax treaty (Corporate Income Tax Act, s 8b, para 2);
- the extension of the participation exemption for both intercompany dividends and capital gains from the disposal of qualifying shares to German branches of non-German companies

acting as "holding branches" (Corporate Income Tax Act, s 8b, para 4);

- the application of the intercompany dividends participation exemption to dividends received by a German corporate shareholder from another German corporation where the dividends are deemed funded out of income which the distributing corporation derived as income exempt from German tax under a tax treaty or under internal German law (Corporate Income Tax Act, s 8b, para 1);
- the elimination of the compensatory corporate income tax levy that was formerly imposed on dividends paid out of treaty-exempt income (Corporate Income Tax Act, s 40, sentence 1, No. 1); and
- the deductibility, subject to certain limitations, of interest on debt incurred in acquiring foreign subsidiary shares (cf. Income Tax Act, s 3c).

As regards personal income tax, Germany's tax rates remain high. However, personal capital gains continue to enjoy complete exemption from tax, provided the two-year holding period for real estate and the six-month holding period for personal property (including portfolio shareholdings) is observed. In the absence of specific ESOP legislation the capital gains exemption plays a major role in designing tax-efficient structures for the participation of management in a holding or operating company.

VIII. LABOUR LAW AND EMPLOYMENT CONSIDERATIONS

1. Individual Labour Law

Contracts of employment must be entered into, or confirmed by the employer, in writing. The Documentation Act (*Nachweisgesetz*) of 20th July 1995 requires that the employer notify the employee in writing of the essential terms of the employment not later than one month after the stipulated commencement of employment. The notification must contain at least ten particulars specified in the Act, including identity of the parties, description of the work, compensation, vacation and applicable notice periods. No such notification is necessary where the parties have entered into a written contract of employment which contains the required ten particulars (s 2). Oral contracts of employment which have been entered into prior to the coming into force of the Documentation Act (28th July 1995) have to be confirmed in writing if so requested by the employee (s 4). The Documentation Act does not contain any sanctions. Non-compliance with the form requirement would not affect the validity of an employment contract.

Contracts of employment which have not been entered into for a fixed period of time can be terminated by either party by giving notice of termination. If nothing to the contrary has been agreed upon between the parties and no applicable collective bargaining agreement provides otherwise, the statutory notice periods have to be observed. The statute no longer distinguishes between blue collar and white collar employees. The uniform notice period for all employees is now four weeks and any termination can only become effective on the 15th day of a calendar month or at the end of a calendar month (Civil Code, s 622, para 1). The statutory notice period applicable to a termination by the employer increases with the length of service of the employee to be terminated (from one month after two years of service to seven months after twenty years of service, the termination to become effective only at the end of a calendar month) (s 622, para 2). No notice periods need be observed where there is serious cause (*wichtiger Grund*) justifying immediate termination.

However, the right of the employer to terminate a contract of employment has been severely restricted by statutory law. The Act against Unfair Dismissals (*Kündigungsschutzgesetz*) in general protects all employees who have been in service with the terminating employer for more than six months, provided the employer employs more than five employees.* Any ordinary termination of a contract of employment with an employee who enjoys protection under the Act is invalid, unless the employer can show that the termination is "socially" justified. As a rule, "social justification" is deemed to exist only if the termination is caused either by reason of the person or behaviour of the employee or by urgent business reasons which prevent the continuation of the employment. The existence of a works council (*Betriebsrat*) will complicate a termination by the employer even further because the works council has to be heard prior to the giving of notice (Shop Constitution Act 1972, s 102, para 1). The employer has to inform the works council about the reasons for a proposed termination. The works council may raise objections but, ultimately, it may not block a termination. Any notice of termination given by the employer without prior involvement of the works council is null and void (s 102, para 1, third sentence). Certain classes of employees, such as works council members, disabled

---

* A bill was introduced in 1996 to increase this number to 10 employees.

employees or pregnant women, enjoy additional protection against termination.

2. Collective Bargaining Agreements
(*Tarifverträge*)

Collective bargaining agreements are negotiated and entered into between individual trade unions on one side and (predominantly) employers' associations or (less frequently) individual employers on the other. The collective bargaining system deals primarily with the adequacy of remuneration of labour at an industry-wide level and reaches its last resort in strike and lock-out. Collective bargaining agreements typically contain provisions as to working hours, vacation and compensation. In general, they are only binding on the members of the trade union and the members of the employers' association (or the individual employers) who entered into the relevant agreements (Collective Bargaining Agreements Act (*Tarifvertragsgesetz*), s 3). However, in practice they usually constitute minimum standards for all employees of the industry to which the contracting trade union belongs, though higher ranking employees will often have contracts providing for better terms. The Federal Minister of Labour can in certain circumstances declare a collective bargaining agreement to be of general application in the industry concerned.

3. Co-Determination (*Mitbestimmung*)

The German labour force plays an active role not only in matters directly related to the terms and conditions of employment but also in questions relating to the operation and organisation of the business as a whole. There are essentially two levels of labour representation where employees and trade unions may exercise their influence on the employers, namely at shop floor level and board level, the latter being ultimately less important.

(a) Shop Floor Level Co-Determination (*Betriebliche Mitbestimmung*)

Under the Shop Constitution Act (*Betriebsverfassungsgesetz*) of 1972, the employees at a workplace (*Betrieb*) with five or more permanent employees are entitled to elect a works council (*Betriebsrat*) (Shop Constitution Act 1972, s 1). Where a company has more than one workplace (e.g. a production facility in one location and administrative offices in a second location) then, in addition to the various local works councils, a combined works council (*Gesamtbetriebsrat*), composed of one or two members of each of the local works councils, has to be established (s 47). If several companies belong to the same group of companies, then the individual companies' works councils (or combined works councils, if any), may decide to establish a group works council (*Konzernbetriebstrat*) (s 54).

Each works council has certain rights of information, consultation and cooperation, veto rights and rights of consent, and other rights of co-determination with regard to a wide range of social matters (plant regulations concerning discipline on the shop floor, behaviour of employees, working hours, terms and method of payment of remuneration, vacation issues etc.), operational matters (working procedures and work methods, installation, establishment of or alterations to manufacturing, administration and other plant facilities), personnel matters (personnel planning, hiring and dismissal of employees) and other economic and financial matters (s 74 *et seq.*).

In enterprises regularly employing more than 100 permanent employees, an economic committee (*Wirtschaftsausschuss*) has to be established in addition to the works council (s 106). The economic committee is composed of employees of the business selected by the works council, one of whom has to be a member of the works council (s 106). The economic committee has the function of discussing economic matters with the employer and of advising the works council about such discussions. The employer has to keep the economic committee informed and to consult with it on all business matters, including the economic and financial condition of the enterprise, the production and marketing situation, the production and investment programme, any planned rationalisations, reductions or close-downs of workplaces or parts thereof, the integration of separate workplaces, changes in the organisation or the purpose of any workplace and any other issues or objectives which may materially affect the interests of the employees. The committee is entitled to detailed and timely information in advance of such events, including the relevant documents.

The law does not provide for mandatory union representatives on works councils or economic committees. However, very often the members of these bodies happen to be union members and the law expressly requires that the employer and works council should work together in mutual confidence assisted by the unions and relevant employer associations to the benefit of the employees and the business as a whole.

(b) Board-Level Co-Determination (*Unternehmerische Mitbestimmung*)

Labour representation at board level is statutorily provided for by four different co-determination acts. They make the creation of a supervisory board mandatory and require that a defined percentage of its members must be employee-elected. The other members continue to be appointed and removed by the shareholders. The four acts are:

(1) The Shop Constitution Act (*Betriebsverfassungsgesetz*) 1952, under which corporations employing more than 500 individuals must have a supervisory board which is composed of one-third of employee-elected members and two-thirds of shareholder-elected or appointed members. An AG established prior to 10th August 1994 is subject to one-third employee representation on the supervisory board even if it has less than 500 employees, unless it qualifies as a so-called family-owned company. In a GmbH the statutory authority of the shareholders' meeting to appoint and remove the managing directors is not affected by this one-third co-determination on the supervisory board.

(2) The Co-Determination Act (*Mitbestimmungsgesetz*) 1976 is applicable to enterprises of certain legal types (in particular corporations such as GmbHs and AGs but, in general, not partnerships) which employ more than 2000 employees. This Act requires that the supervisory board of such companies should consist of an equal number of shareholders' and labour representatives. However, shareholder majority is nevertheless guaranteed because, in the event of a tie, the chairman, who is elected by the shareholders, has the casting vote. The management board must be appointed and can only be removed by the supervisory board and must have one member who is in charge of labour and social matters (*Arbeitsdirektor*). Unlike the Act on Co-Determination in the Coal, Iron and Steel Industry, the Co-Determination Act does not give weighted influence to the labour side with respect to the appointment and removal of the labour director.

(3) The Act on Co-Determination in the Coal, Iron and Steel Industry (*Montan-Mitbestimmungsgesetz*) 1951 (historically the first Co-Determination Act) provides for special rules with regard to the composition of the supervisory board of enterprises in the coal, iron and steel industries. The supervisory board of qualifying enterprises has to be composed of an equal number of shareholders' and employees' representatives as well as of so-called "additional members" who are supposed to be "neutral" and to

function as tie breakers. This supervisory board has exclusive authority to appoint and remove the members of the management board. The Act further requires that the management board has one member who is in charge of labour and social matters (*Arbeitsdirektor*) and who cannot be appointed and removed without the approval of the majority of the employees' representatives.

(4) The basic principles of the above Act have been extended to certain holding companies which own enterprises in the coal, iron and steel industries by the Supplementary Coal, Iron and Steel Co-Determination Act (*Montan-Mitbestimmungsergänzungsgesetz*) 1956.

The influence afforded by these co-determination acts to employees is not as significant as it might at first appear, since supervisory boards decide by majority vote. The Shop Constitution Act provides for one third employee representation only, while the other three acts, though providing for equal employee and shareholder representation, give the chairman (a shareholder representative) or the "neutral" member the casting vote in tie situations. Moreover, the function of the supervisory board consists primarily of the supervision of the management board and it has no managerial rights. The labour side can, of course, try to influence the composition of the management board where the power to appoint and remove the management board is vested in the supervisory board.

None of the co-determination acts provides for employee representation at the management board level. Although some of the acts require that one member of the board of directors should be a labour director (*Arbeitsdirektor*) with specific responsibilities for social and labour matters, the labour director is not an employee representative but has a position equivalent to that of the other directors. Nevertheless, the mere representation of the labour side on the supervisory board level impacts on the decision process of the management board. Management tends to discuss critical issues informally with the employee representatives, who often are also members of the works council, in order to avoid conflicts on the board and in the business in general. This affords the labour side the possibility of obtaining information, making their views known and considered and, ultimately, influencing the course of business.

4. Particular Aspects Relative to Acquisitions

(a) Share Transaction

If an acquisition is structured as a share transaction, the identity of the employer remains unchanged. This is true for the acquisition of both shares in a corporation and interests in a partnership. A share deal will neither affect existing employment relationships, nor any of the mutual rights and duties under existing labour contracts.

A share transaction is, in general, not subject to any co-determination or participation rights of the works council, except for an obligation to inform the economic committee in due time before the transaction is consummated (Shop Constitution Act 1972, s 106, para 2).

(b) Asset Transaction

(1) *Transfer of Employment Contracts*
A different regime applies in an asset transaction where the employers before and after the transaction are different legal entities. In this case, all employment contracts pertaining to the business acquired normally transfer to the purchaser as a matter of law.

Section 613a of the Civil Code provides that if a business (*Betrieb*) or a part of a business (*Betriebsteil*) is transferred to a new owner, all employment relationships, including all rights and obligations under the various employment contracts, which were in existence at the time of the transfer and pertaining to the business or the part of the business transferred should pass to the new owner by operation of law. The parties cannot contract out of this provision.

A business (*Betrieb*) is defined as an organisationally independent unit within which an employer continuously pursues certain business purposes using material, intangible and human resources. A part of a business (*Betriebsteil*) is an organisational sub-unit pursuing a partial activity within the overall business purpose. Typically, a plant, a division or a department will qualify as a part of a business.

It is not necessary that each and every asset of a business or part of a business be transferred in order to trigger the applicability of s 613a of the Civil Code. A transfer of an essential part of the assets is sufficient if the purchaser is enabled thereby to continue the business. On the other hand, a transfer of individual assets which are of minor import-ance for the conduct of the business (e.g. a machine) will not qualify under the section. However, in a more recent decision, the European Court of Justice held that the outsourcing of services (in the case at hand: the transfer of cleaning work performed by one single employee to another company) could qualify as a transfer of a business even if no assets were transferred, provided that the "economic identity" of the business is preserved.*

Section 613a of the Civil Code leads to an automatic transfer only with regard to existing employment relationships. Only true employees will pass over to the purchaser. Members of the management board of an AG and managing directors of a GmbH, for instance, are not considered as true employees and consequently do not qualify for an automatic transfer. Former employees, whose employment was terminated prior to the acquisition, do not pass over either, even if they have vested pension rights. The same is true for pensioners. However, the purchaser may become liable for claims of former employees and pensioners under s 25 of the Commercial Code if he continues to carry the firm name of the seller, or under s 419 of the Civil Code if he acquires all or substantially all of the assets of the seller. (Section 419 of the Civil Code has been repealed with effect from 1st January 1999.)

The purchaser assumes by operation of law all rights and obligations under the contracts of employment of the employees passing over to him, including the obligation to pay old age benefits (whether they are vested or not). Collective rights resulting from collective bargaining agreements or plant agreements are transformed into individual rights and barred from unilateral changes for one year if such issues are not collectively regulated in the buyer's workplace. If there are such collective regulations in the buyer's workplace, these regulations will substitute for the old regulations automatically. The assumption of employment obligations by the purchaser is particularly important with regard to any pension rights enjoyed by the employees transferred, since this assumption may result in a considerable financial burden for the purchaser, perhaps jeopardising the entire acquisition. At the least it is likely to influence the purchase price. The seller is jointly and severally liable with the purchaser for employment-related obligations which were created prior to the transfer and which become due within one year after the transfer.

The transfer of employment relationships takes place automatically by operation of law. However, according to legal precedent each employee is individually entitled to object to the transfer. In this event, the contract of employment remains in force with the seller, but the seller may be entitled to terminate the contract of employment if there is no

---

European Court of Justice, decision of 14th April 1994, ZIP 1994, 1036 ("Christel Schmidt"*). The court considers such "economic identity" to be in particular preserved if the same or a similar business activity can be continued or resumed by the new owner.

longer any suitable job for the objecting employee. An employee may also give his express or implied consent to the transfer of employment, thus waiving his right to object. This can be done before or after the transfer of the business. The period available to an employee to decide whether to consent or to object is normally about three weeks. An employee who does not raise an objection within such period or who continues to work for the new employer without making any reservations although he is aware that the business has actually transferred is deemed to have given his consent to the transfer of his employment. If it is crucial for the purchaser not only to acquire assets but also certain key personnel, the purchaser should make sure, prior to the closing, that the particular employees concerned give their consent to the transfer. This can be done by giving timely information to the employees and fixing a time limit for any objections.

Section 613a of the Civil Code constitutes mandatory law. The seller and the purchaser of a business or part of a business cannot agree that the employees pertaining thereto or part of them will not pass to the purchaser. Neither the seller nor the purchaser can terminate or unilaterally modify employment contracts because of or in connection with the transfer. However, a termination of a contract of employment is valid if effected by agreement with the individual employee(s), provided such agreements are not collectively used to circumvent the intent of the Code. Compensation for the waiver of pension rights is, even with the express consent of the employees concerned, subject to narrow restrictions.

Although s 613a of the Civil Code constitutes mandatory law, the seller and the buyer can and often will agree on provisions in the acquisition contract which supplement or even deviate from the statutory concept. Typically, those provisions address the following issues:

- representations by the seller as to the correctness and completeness of information given on employees (in particular concerning specification and compensation of employees transferring);
- termination of employees by the seller prior to the closing;
- payment of compensation for employees involuntarily taken over by the buyer;
- impact of pension liabilities to be assumed by the buyer on the purchase price;
- information of the workforce in order to trigger the right of employees to object to the transfer of employment;
- consequences of objections by employees to the transfer of employment;

- representation by the seller or closing condition that objections by employees will not exceed a certain percentage and/or that certain key employees will not object;

Provisions which are in conflict with s 613a of the Civil Code have no direct effect on the position of the employees concerned but are binding among the parties to the acquisition contract.

(2) Co-Determination

A transfer of a business or part of a business has, as a rule, to be reported to the relevant economic committees (Shop Constitution Act 1972, s 106, para 2). In the first place, the seller will have to inform his own economic committee. It is conceivable that the purchaser may also have to inform his economic committee, if any, where the target corporation is to be integrated into an existing business. The information has to be given in a timely manner before the transfer is effected.

The transfer of a business as such is not subject to any co-determination rights of the works council. In many cases however, particularly if only part of a business is being transferred, the transfer will constitute a so-called operational change (*Betriebsänderung*) under s 111 of the Shop Constitution Act of 1972, resulting in a right of the seller's works council to negotiate with the seller a compromise of interest (*Interessenausgleich*) in order to structure the measures to be taken in the course of the transaction, and a social plan (*Sozialplan*) under which adverse effects for the employees concerned are financially compensated or mitigated.

If no agreement can be reached between employer and the works council, a conciliation board (*Einigungsstelle*) has to be established, consisting of an equal number of employer and employee representatives with a neutral chairman. The chairman can either be appointed by mutual selection of the parties or by a labour court upon the motion of one party. The appointment of the chairman by a labour court is subject to an appeal procedure so that the works council has ample opportunities to delay the conclusion of a compromise of interest and social plan although it cannot prevent the operational change, since any suggestion of the conciliation board concerning the compromise of interest is not binding on the employer.

After the employer has exhausted the various procedural steps, he can ignore the suggestions of the conciliation board and maintain his own original plan. By using legitimate delaying tactics, the works council can, however, improve its bargaining position in relation to the social plan negotiations. The ruling of the conciliation board on the social plan is final and is not subject to judicial review, except in the case of abuse of discretion by the board (which can hardly ever be established and proven). As a rule, financial compensation for loss of employment can range between one half and one month's gross payment per year of service per employee.

IX. NEGOTIATING THE ACQUISITION CONTRACT

1. General Background

Acquiring successfully in Germany requires an approach adapted to the German environment and practice. An aggressive Anglo-American acquisition style may cause the envisaged takeover to fail.

In large-scale transactions, where the seller auctions off the company or where the purchaser submits a public tender offer, the Anglo-American approach might work. But those transactions are relatively rare in Germany. The vast majority of deals are privately negotiated acquisitions of small and medium-sized private firms which are often family owned. These transactions demand a high degree of sensitivity, diplomacy, persuasive bargaining and, sometimes, patience.

A major difficulty for the potential buyer is often to persuade the owner to sell and to be seriously considered as a purchaser. A private owner normally has a strong emotional attachment to his business and is less rational than an employed manager. He feels loyal to his employees and wants to maintain his reputation within his local community and social environment. The owner will refuse a sale that might be perceived as the result of a personal failure. The price offered for the target is certainly an important inducement for the owner to part with his business, but monetary gain is by no means decisive. The owner has to be convinced that the purchaser is sympathetic, fair and reasonable, has a viable strategy and makes a long-term commitment, in other words, that the business will be "in good hands" when transferred to the purchaser.

Once contacts have been established, the initial negotiations should be conducted at the top level with the involvement of very few people only. Large negotiating teams of the buyer act as a deterrent. Lengthy due diligence checklists and large investigation teams are often viewed as an affront. The buyer should consider that the proposed transaction might be a once in a lifetime event for the owner and that the owner (and sometimes even his adviser) might have little to no experience in M&A practice. The buyer should also be cautious when he submits his first draft of the acquisition agreement. Although the once prevalent acquisition agreements with only few pages have made way to more complex contracts, German sellers still have a distinct distaste for over-elaborate agreements. There is in general little readiness to give representations and warranties to the extent customary in US agreements. The signing of the acquisition agreement and the closing of the transaction normally coincide under German practice. To propose a separate closing, which is supposed to take place some time after the signing and which is subject to a number of closing conditions, will be received with a high degree of distrust on the part of the seller.

No reasonable foreign buyer will carry out an acquisition in Germany without local legal advice. But experience shows that such advice is sometimes confined strictly to issues of local law and not sought (or not followed) with regard to the particularities of the local environment and practice. This is a mistake which is likely to result in aggravation and frustration on both sides of the transaction, to complicate and strain the negotiation process and, maybe, even jeopardise the entire deal.

2. Due Diligence

It has become common practice that a purchaser carries out a due diligence investigation of the business before acquiring it. The extent and the timing of such an investigation is a matter of agreement between the parties and varies from case to case.

A due diligence investigation inevitably exposes a conflict of interest between the seller and the buyer. The seller does not want to disclose details about the target before he is certain that the purchaser will actually go through with the acquisition. This is a legitimate interest because an investigation results in expenditures, it may alarm the workforce and it may even make known sensitive business information to a competitor. The buyer, on the other hand, does not want to be bound until he knows whether the business is exactly what he expected.

The seller will be less reluctant to give the buyer access to the business once a letter of intent has been signed. Although a letter of intent is in general not binding, it raises the likelihood that the buyer is serious about the acquisition. In addition, the seller will normally request the buyer to undertake to treat information acquired in the due diligence process as confidential. Such a confidentiality agreement is often part of a letter of intent (which is then binding insofar), but it is also often found as a separate contract. The Anglo-American technique of separating the signing of the acquisition agreement from the closing of the transaction, having the due diligence investigation carried out during the interim period between signing and closing and giving the buyer a practically unrestricted right to refuse the closing and walk away from the acquisition, is rarely applied in Germany. This technique does not give the seller the required certainty that the purchase will actually be completed. Only if the acquisition agreement provides for a clear-cut obligation of the buyer to close if specific formal and precisely defined closing conditions have been fulfilled (e.g. approvals by authorities or third parties have been obtained) will the seller consider such an approach.

The due diligence investigation is designed to give the purchaser an understanding of the commercial, financial and legal aspects of the business. What is required therefor depends on the particular circumstances, such as the type of business (e.g. production or service) and the ownership structure (e.g. family-owned or public), as well as on the familiarity of the purchaser with the business and the relevant industry. A due diligence investigation is no routine procedure which can be carried out following some standard checklist. A standard checklist may serve as a starting point, but it has to be specifically tailored to the target under consideration. Considerable aggravation on the part of the seller can be avoided if such adaptation takes place before the checklist is submitted.

3. Obligation to Negotiate in Good Faith

The mere entering into negotiations between the seller and the purchaser establishes a pre-contractual relationship which imposes various obligations on the parties, regardless of whether or not an acquisition agreement is eventually signed. These obligations have been broadly defined to comprise duties of mutual consideration, care and loyalty resulting from the trust requested and provided by the parties. A negligent or intentional violation of a pre-contractual obligation by the seller or the buyer may result in a claim for damages by the other party, provided that it has actually suffered damage (principle of *culpa in contrahendo* or *Verschulden bei Vertragsschluss*).

A wide body of case law has developed which defines in greater detail sets of pre-contractual obligations. In the context of acquisitions, each party is required to negotiate in good faith. Incorrect or misleading statements, in particular with regard to material financial data, such as balance sheets, profit and loss statements or profitability, are likely to constitute a violation of such duty. The same holds true for the non-disclosure of material information which, as the non-disclosing party is aware, is relevant to the other party's decision to enter into the transaction and which a party negotiating in good faith would normally disclose.

The pre-contractual obligation to negotiate in good faith does not, as such, require any party to sign the acquisition agreement and close the transaction. As long as no binding commitment has been made, either party may in principle walk away from the negotiations without becoming liable for damages. However, where a party has caused the other party to believe that the contract will definitely be signed, in particular when agreement has been reached on all terms and conditions, breaking off negotiations without reasonable cause may give rise to a claim for damages by the other side. The damage to be compensated would comprise any damages suffered by relying on the consummation of the contract, e.g. out of pocket expenses and damages suffered by not pursuing a realistic alternative transaction (but not lost profit under the contract in question).

4. Letter of Intent and Pre-Contract

Once the negotiations have resulted in a basic agreement on the major business and legal points, the parties will often reduce their understanding to writing in a more or less summary fashion. The document drawn up in this connection may have different designations, such as "letter of intent" (*Absichtserklärung*), "memorandum", "memorandum of understanding", "heads of agreement" or "pre-contract" (*Vorvertrag*). Whether or not such a document constitutes a binding commitment on the parties to enter into a definitive acquisition agreement is a matter of construction of the relevant document.

The crucial question is whether both parties expressly or impliedly expressed their intention that the document be binding. The answer to this question has to be given based on all relevant facts of the case. The designation of the document may constitute an indication but is not decisive. The designation as "letter of intent" normally supports the view that the parties did not have the intention to be bound. On the other hand, if the parties have chosen to designate their document as "pre-contract" (*Vorvertrag*), this strongly speaks for an intended contractual commitment.

Section 154 of the Civil Code provides for two rebuttable presumptions in this connection, which will apply in case of doubt. First, as long as the parties have not reached agreement on all items of a contract on which agreement was to be reached according to the request of at least one party, there is no binding contract. Second, where the parties have agreed to notarise their agreement, no binding contract exists before the notarisation has taken place. Of course, if the agreement has to be notarised by law, a binding contract can be created only by notarisation.

A document drawn up by the parties early in the negotiation process may also include a confidentiality clause (although most sophisticated sellers will insist on a separate, upfront confidentiality agreement), a clause regarding the exclusivity of the negotiations as well as provisions covering costs and limitations of liability if a party decides to break off the negotiations. Because it is doubtful whether and, if so, to which extent such a document is binding, it is advisable that the parties address this issue and state expressly in the document which of its provisions are meant to be binding (and for how long) and which are not.

5. Important Elements of Contract

The factual, legal and tax issues as well as the interests of the seller and the purchaser differ in each acquisition. Each transaction follows its own rules and there is no such thing as a standard acquisition agreement. Nevertheless, there are a number of issues which are typically dealt with in an acquisition contract or which should at least be considered when drawing up the contract. The following is a checklist of important items typically covered in an acquisition contract.

(a) Parties

Sometimes, the negotiations will be conducted by parties other than the eventual seller and purchaser, e.g. when groups of companies are concerned and the parent companies are negotiating agreements to be entered into by subsidiaries, or when the purchaser is newly established, or when the parties switch from a share deal to an asset deal, or vice versa. In any case, the contracting parties must be precisely designated. If either of them is not adequately credit-worthy, guarantees may be requested from third parties, such as shareholders or banks.

(b) Subject Matter

The subject matter of the acquisition has to be precisely defined. In particular, it must be specified whether the deal is structured as an asset transaction, a share transaction or a combination of both.

In an asset transaction, the assets and liabilities to be transferred must be precisely specified. Reference merely to a balance sheet will often not suffice because non-activated rights and agreements will also have to be transferred. It should be remembered that agreements and liabilities, in general, cannot be transferred without the third party's consent, that employment agreements may pass over to the purchaser by operation of law and that the purchaser, again by operation of law, may become liable for the debts of the seller.

In a share transaction, the shares or interests to be transferred must be precisely specified. This is also true for any ancillary rights pertaining to the shares and interests respectively. When interests in a partnership are sold, it is important to address the issue of whether *all* partnership accounts of the seller (e.g. loan account, capital reserve account, capital account II, private account) are to be transferred and whether the seller is to be entitled to make any withdrawals between the signing and the transfer date.

The contract should spell out who is entitled to the profit of the company for which period. In this regard, the question of who is entitled to prepare and determine the underlying accounts should also be considered, and also, whether the other party should be given a right to participate in that process. Moreover, it is recommended that the issue of tax audits for periods prior to the transfer date be addressed as well as their consequences for the allocation of profits.

(c) Closing and Transfer Date

In the Anglo-American practice "closing" (or "completion") describes the final steps of the transaction whereby the previously signed acquisition agreement is consummated. The closing takes place at a date ("closing date") agreed upon by the parties in the acquisition agreement or after the signing of the agreement. The acquisition agreement specifies the acts to be carried out at the closing, which include in particular the legal transfer of the business, the payment of the purchase price, the exchange of documents such as resignation letters by board members, third party consents, accountant reports and (rarely) legal opinions, the assignment of shareholder loans and the repetition of representations and warranties.

German acquisition agreements do not traditionally provide for a closing. The acts normally carried out at a closing are largely part of the acquisition agreement and performed at the signing of such agreement. In general, the transfer of the business (assets or shares) is effected in and by the acquisition agreement, but subject to the condition precedent that the seller has received payment of the purchase price. To put it differently, in a German-style acquisition agreement signing and closing typically coincide. A separate closing, however, has proved to be useful in large complex transactions and to be practically unavoidable in international cross-border transactions. Even so, the typical German seller is not prepared to accept closing conditions which would leave it at the discretion of the purchaser whether or not the closing takes place.

If there is a separate closing and the period between the signing and the closing is longer than just a few days, the purchaser will request that the seller be contractually restricted in the conduct of the business. The parties will often agree that certain business decisions taken during such interim period require the consent of the purchaser. In cases where the transaction is subject to mandatory pre-merger control so that it must not be completed prior to regulatory approval, it is legally problematic to provide for such a consent requirement because, depending on its scope, it may give the purchaser control over the business and might be considered therefore as an effective con-summation of the acquisition for purposes of antitrust law.

The transfer date is the date on which the transfer of the business sold becomes effective for purposes of the internal relationship between the parties. On such date the risks and benefits of the business sold are deemed to pass from the seller to the purchaser. In an asset transaction, the transfer date serves as cutoff date for the allocation of profits and losses, costs, liabilities and the like and the allocation is often carried out on the basis of a balance sheet established as per the transfer date.

Typically, the transfer date will coincide with the closing date or, if there is no separate closing, with the date of signing, i.e. when the legal transfer of the business takes place. But this is not mandatory and the parties may agree otherwise. A retroactive transfer is legally not possible. However, the parties may approximate a retroactive transfer by agreeing to put themselves in the position they would have been in if the transfer had taken place at a specified earlier date. Taxwise, a retroactive transfer will not be recognised in general. When interests in a partnership are being sold, for tax purposes the selling partners will always be deemed to have received the profit attributable to their interests up to the date of the actual legal transfer of such interests.

(d) Purchase Price

The purchase price may be fixed or variable (in particular depending on the net equity or earnings shown in accounts prepared as at the closing date, the transfer date or some different date). The purchase price may also be entirely unspecified and expressed only by reference to a formula set out in the contract, such as in earn-out arrangements.

The time and mode of payment as well as any adjustment mechanism have to be addressed. In the case of payment by instalments, the parties will usually agree that interest is payable and the seller is normally granted security. Quite often, the contract will provide for a retention of the purchase price or part thereof for a specified period of time (e.g. until the establishment of a closing balance sheet or until the expiration of any limitation period applicable to claims under the warranties).

If the seller has granted loans to the business sold, the question needs to be addressed whether the seller will assign the loans to the purchaser and, if so, whether the purchase price includes the compensation for the assignment.

(e) Representations and Warranties

It is customary for the seller to represent and warrant the existence or non-existence of a variety of facts, circumstances and relationships. The purchaser usually wants the list of such terms to be as complete as possible, whereas the seller typically wishes to sell on an "as is" basis. The scope of the representations and warranties ultimately stipulated in the contract will depend, of course, to a large extent on the bargaining power of the parties. Quite often, individual sellers in Germany are not prepared to give the kind of extensive representations and warranties frequently found in Anglo-American acquisition contracts. Representations and warranties by the purchaser hardly ever occur.

(f) Legal Remedies

German law on contracts is not designed for the acquisition of businesses. As a consequence, it is not clear on the legal remedies available to the purchaser if the business is different from what he could expect. For this reason, the parties should provide explicitly and exhaustively in the contract what remedies the purchaser should have in the event that the seller does not deliver as promised, in particular if any representation or warranty given by the seller turns out to be incorrect. Under statutory law, a breach of a warranty (or guarantee) will in general give the purchaser the option to reduce the purchase price, rescind the acquisition agreement or claim damages for non-performance. These rights are often impracticable and mostly contracted out. The standard remedy provided for instead is the obligation of the seller to put the purchaser and the target in the position in which they would have been if the warranty had been correct. This comes close to an indemnification and hold harmless obligation customary in the Anglo-American practice. If the purchaser is granted a right of rescission, it is usually limited to serious cases, in particular where the business turns out to be bankrupt, unprofitable or otherwise of no interest to the purchaser or where the seller has fraudulently concealed defects of the business.

(g) Statute of Limitations

The statutory periods of limitation after which the claims of the purchaser will become barred may range, depending on the nature of the claim, between six months and 30 years. The parties usually look for a uniform period of limitation for all types of claims. A period between two and four years, starting from the date of transfer, is quite customary. Insofar as items reflected in a balance sheet are concerned, it is a rule of thumb that the purchaser should have the opportunity to draw up balance sheets for two consecutive business years after the acquisition before his claims become barred. An exception should be made for remedies the purchaser may have as a result of undisclosed tax liabilities relating to the business. The statute of limitation for such remedies should start to run only after the tax assessment for the relevant period prior to the transfer date has become final. An exception may also be appropriate for remedies of the purchaser in connection with claims of third parties, environmental liabilities and in cases of fraud.

(h) Covenant not to Compete

The seller will often undertake not to compete with the business sold. The scope of such a covenant and the consequences in case of violation must be clearly defined. Antitrust and tax aspects should also be considered.

(i) Participation of Parties in Legal Proceedings, Tax Audits and Merger Control Proceedings

Depending on the agreement reached in the acquisition contract, the outcome of legal proceedings and tax audits may have an effect on the party not directly involved therein. Acquisition contracts, therefore, often provide that the party affected shall be entitled to participate in such legal proceedings or tax audits. In merger control proceedings, it is common practice for the parties to co-ordinate their approach towards the Federal Cartel Office; an equivalent obligation is, as a result, frequently found in acquisition contracts.

(j) Arbitration or Place of Venue

If the parties want disputes to be resolved by an arbitration tribunal, rather than by the ordinary courts, they enter into an arbitration agreement. An arbitration agreement, in general, has to be laid down in a separate document signed by both parties which must not contain any agreements other than those relating to the arbitration proceedings. An exception to this requirement of form applies only if both parties are "full" merchants (*Vollkaufleute*) for whom the arbitration agreement constitutes a commercial transaction. Because in the case of natural persons it is often difficult to assess whether the prerequisites of this exception are fulfilled, it is advisable to draw up a separate arbitration agreement.

If the parties want disputes to be decided upon by the ordinary courts, they will normally provide for a specific court to have jurisdiction. However, such a provision is, in general, only enforceable against merchants.

(k) Taxes and Costs

The contract should provide which party has to bear any transfer taxes (i.e. value added tax and, possibly, real estate transfer tax) and costs (e.g. for legal advisers, notaries, administrative proceedings, brokers) arising in connection with the transaction. Unless provision to the contrary has been made in the contract, the costs of delivery of tangible assets as well as the costs of creation and transfer of rights have to be borne by the seller.

(l) Governing Law

The law governing the acquisition contract should be specified if one party is non-German or if the contract involves any other foreign aspects, whether of a factual or legal nature.

6. Formal Requirements

(a) Form of Contract; Notarisation

(1) *General*

An acquisition contract does not in general require any particular form. Under certain circumstances, however, the contract must be in notarial form (*Beurkundung*) in order to be valid. This means that the parties or their proxies have to appear before a notary public (*Notar*) and that the document must be read aloud to the parties in a formal procedure. Notarial form for the acquisition agreement is required by statute in the following important cases:

- asset transactions involving the conveyance of real estate;
- transactions in which a natural or legal person agrees to transfer all of its assets;
- transactions involving the transfer of shares in a GmbH.

Where notarisation is required, this formal requirement generally extends to the entire transaction. If an asset transaction, for instance, involves the sale of real estate, the entire acquisition agreement, including any side agreements (e.g. service contracts, arbitration agreements), must be in notarial form. "Side-letters" which have not been notarised jeopardise the validity of the entire transaction. It is not possible to split the transaction into single agreements and to notarise only the sale of real estate.

An undertaking to transfer or acquire real estate which has not been properly notarised (and which is, therefore, not enforceable), becomes effective when the transfer of title is registered in the real estate register. This validation effect covers the entire transaction and even extends to side agreements. The same principle applies with regard to shares in a GmbH. A properly notarised transfer of shares validates any lack of notarisation of the underlying undertaking to transfer the shares.

Quite often, the parties make use of this principle by merely signing (rather than notarising) the acquisition agreement containing the commitment to transfer shares and then notarising only the actual transfer of the shares. This technique can save considerable time because it avoids the time-consuming notarisation of the whole (typically lengthy) acquisition agreement. It can also save money where the transaction value of the acquisition agreement is higher than the value of the shares. This technique is acceptable to the parties, however, only in cases where the time span between the signing of the acquisition agreement and the actual transfer of the shares (validating the invalidity of the acquisition agreement) is relatively short, so that there is no long period of uncertainty during which either party could walk away from the agreement.

(2) *Notarisation Abroad*
Notarisation in Germany does not come cheap. The fees of German notaries are set by statute in relation to the value of the transaction.

For the transfer of a share, for instance, the transaction value is equal to the fair market value of the share. If only the share transfer is notarised, a transaction value of DM1m results in notarial fees of DM3220, a transaction value of DM10m in fees of DM30,220, a transaction value of DM100m in fees of DM103,020 and a transaction value of DM1bn in fees of DM142,020, in each case plus value added tax. The parties sometimes consider having the contract notarised abroad by a notary who is less expensive than a German notary or avoiding notarisation altogether by subjecting the contract to a foreign law or executing it in a foreign country which does not require notarisation. This is not without risk, though.

German conflict of law rules provide that a contract is valid as to form if it fulfils the formal requirements either of the law by which it is governed or of the law of the country in which it is entered into (Introductory Act to the Civil Code (*EGBGB*), article 11). Under these rules, real estate located in Germany could be effectively sold (but not transferred) in France, for instance, without observing the German law requirement of notarisation. Whether these rules can also be relied upon in transactions involving shares in a GmbH is highly controversial and has not yet been decided by the Federal Supreme Court. Prudence would dictate having a share transaction notarised.

This raises the next question, namely whether notarisation by a non-German notary fulfils the requirement of notarial form under German law. There is no clear answer to this question either. With regard to GmbH shares, the prevailing opinion acknowledges the sufficiency of notarisation by non-German notaries, provided that their legal education, professional standing and recording procedure is equivalent to that of a German notary. This equivalence is acknowledged, again by the prevailing opinion, in the case of most Swiss notaries (depending on the canton) and Austrian notaries, but not in the case of US notaries. Because of the controversy surrounding this issue, a risk-averse party will go the safe route and insist on notarisation in Germany, albeit at higher costs. The transfer of German real estate (*Auflassung*) must always be recorded by a German notary in order to be valid.

(b) Consents and Approvals

The acquisition of a business may require consents or approvals both under civil and public law. The most important examples are:

- Where the acquisition is subject to mandatory pre-merger control, it may not be completed without prior approval of the Federal Cartel Office or the EU Commission.

- If both parties to an agreement are residents or domiciled in Germany, a payment stipulation which provides for a currency other than Deutsche mark must in general be approved by the Federal Bank (*Bundesbank*) in order to be valid. The invalidity of the payment stipulation may jeopardise the validity of the entire agreement. The same holds true for clauses whereunder payment is index linked.
- Where a public licence is required for the operation of a business, whether or not the acquisition requires the approval of the licensing authority or whether the acquiror has to apply for a new licence, will depend on the nature of the licence and the structure of the acquisition.
- A married individual living in the statutory matrimonial relationship (*Güterstand der Zugewinngemeinschaft*) and selling all or practically all of his or her assets can validly do so only with the consent of his or her spouse.
- A minor involved in an acquisition must be represented by his parents who, in turn, may often need the consent of the guardian court (*Vormundschaftsgericht*).
- A variety of restrictions under inheritance law have to be considered if the business to be acquired is part of an estate. If an executor has been appointed, the heirs may require his consent or the executor may require the heirs' consent to a disposal of the business.
- A contract by which an AG or KGaA undertakes to transfer the whole of its assets and liabilities only becomes effective upon the consent of its shareholders' meeting. The consent of the shareholders' meeting is also necessary where the essential business assets of the corporation are being transferred.
- Any transfer of interests in a partnership requires the consent of all partners, which may be granted on a general or individual basis. The transfer of shares in a GmbH may be subject to the fulfilment of certain requirements, such as the consent of all shareholders, the company or its management. The transfer of shares in an AG may require the consent of the company.
- Contracts can only be transferred with the consent of all contract parties. The assignability of claims and rights without the approval of the debtor may have been excluded. Liabilities can only be transferred with the consent of the creditor.

(c) Registration

An acquisition agreement does not need to be registered or filed in order to be valid. Indeed, there is no office or authority which would accept such an agreement for registration or filing. Major acquisitions, however, must in general be notified to the Federal Cartel Office in Berlin or the EU Commission in Brussels for the purposes of merger control (see pp. 46–55 above).

X. ACQUISITIONS IN EASTERN GERMANY

1. Background

On 3rd October 1990, the German unification was formally completed by the accession of the German Democratic Republic (GDR) to the Federal Republic of Germany. The territory of the former GDR was transformed into the so-called Five New States of the Federal Republic. The unification resulted, in principle, in the immediate extension of the entire legal system of West Germany — including the law of the EU — to the whole of Germany. For legal, economic and practical reasons, a number of exceptions to this rule had to be made which are mostly, however, of a transitional nature.

2. The Treuhandanstalt

By 1st July 1990, virtually all former East German state enterprises had been transformed into either GmbHs or AGs. A government agency (the *Treuhandanstalt*) had been founded to become their sole direct or indirect shareholder. The Treuhandanstalt was mandated by statute to restructure the East German economy, to turn around and privatise its enterprises, to promote investments and, at the same time, to avoid mass unemployment. Despite some criticism, it has disposed of its task in a remarkably successful and efficient manner. By the end of March 1994 it had privatised 13,960 businesses, secured some 1,500,000 job guarantees and obtained commitments for investments in an amount of more than DM190bn. The cost for this achievement was a staggering DM217bn (primarily for covering the debts of East German companies and their operating and restructuring costs) of which some DM49bn could be recovered through sales. The Treuhandanstalt was dissolved by the end of 1994 and only about 100 companies remained for privatisation at that time.

3. Particularities of Acquisitions

Acquisitions in the Five New States are not very different from those in the rest of Germany. There are a few peculiarities, though, which stem to some extent from the political mandate of the Treuhandanstalt.

During the privatisation phase, the Treuhandanstalt had to dismiss large portions of the workforce and secure substantial capital injections in order to render the notoriously overstaffed former state enterprises competitive and to initiate the necessary modernisation process. At the same time, it had to fight attempts by West German companies to take over East German businesses only to shut them down for competitive reasons or to speculate in real estate. The attainment of high purchase prices was of no priority in this phase. Typically, the Treuhandanstalt would expect the prospective investor to submit a viable business concept for the enterprise to be acquired, in particular addressing the size of the workforce to be maintained and the investments to be made over time. The cornerstones of the business concept would then be reflected in the privatisation agreement by way of employment guarantees, investment guarantees, clauses restricting asset stripping etc. The agency's reluctance to give more than minimum representations and warranties as well as its somewhat bureaucratic decision-making structures have sometimes been a source of concern.

After almost all businesses have been privatised, investors will no longer have to deal with the Treuhandanstalt but rather buy from the new private owners. Nevertheless, the parameters established by the Treuhandanstalt may impact on the terms of a subsequent acquisition, in particular if the privatisation agreement with the Treuhandanstalt has not been completely fulfilled. Some of the more important aspects which continue to characterise an acquisition in Eastern Germany are the following:

(a) Legal History of Target

Many companies in the Five New States were established by way of reorganisation, merger or split-up. In the somewhat chaotic years after the unification, these transactions were not always handled correctly and may even be invalid. As a consequence, the target company may not own all the assets shown on its balance sheet or be liable for debts of other companies not shown on its balance sheet. Risk in this area may be minimised by a thorough check on the legal history of the target.

(b) Restitution

An investor has to consider the possibility of claims for restitution by owners of real estate or businesses expropriated before the unification. Expropriations after World War II were mostly carried out without adequate financial compensation or by abuse of power or by other illegal means. The same is true for expropriations after 1933 during the Third Reich. The general rule of law has been adopted that the rightful owner who lost his property due to such expropriations under the communist East German government or as a result of persecutions during the Third Reich may chose between financial compensation and restitution.*

Experience has shown that restitution claims have mostly concerned real estate of individuals. They have not played a significant role in connection with the acquisition of businesses. Claims for restitution are statute barred by now if they had not been filed before the end of 1992. Moreover, due to various exceptions, an investor's risk of being exposed to such claims has been further considerably reduced. The so-called "investment priority decree" (*Investitionsvorrangbescheid*) has proved to be the most important exception in practice. Such decree may be obtained in special administrative proceedings when an investor undertakes to make a particular investment which merits priority over the restitution claim of the former owner. The decree effectively excludes the claim for restitution and obliges the investor to carry out the promised investment within a fixed timeframe. The former owner is limited to monetary compensation.

(c) After-Effects of Privatisation

In many of its privatisation agreements, the Treuhandanstalt has imposed temporary restrictions on the buyer in order to safeguard the goals pursued in the privatisation process. These restrictions, which were of course reflected in the purchase price payable by the buyer, may affect the conditions of a resale:

- In privatisations of major businesses, the Treuhandanstalt may have accepted the buyer only because of his peculiar credit and standing. Under those circumstances, the privatisation agreement will provide that any sale of the business to another buyer requires the consent of the Treuhandanstalt.
- The buyer may be obliged vis-à-vis the Treuhandanstalt to make certain investments in the acquired business or to employ a certain minimum number of employees therein. Non-fulfilment of these obligations is typically subject to penalties. In a resale situation, the buyer will try to pass on these obligations to the acquirer.

---

* Expropriations under the Soviet military rule between 1945 and 1949 shall not be reversed, however, and entitle only to claims for compensation.

- The privatisation agreement may require that the buyer turn over to the Treuhandanstalt any capital gains from a resale of the business or major assets of the business. This, too, may affect the terms of a resale agreement.

(d) Employment Issues

The statutory rules protecting employees against dismissal and restricting mass lay-offs are almost identical in Western and Eastern Germany. Contrary to perceptions sometimes encountered, this does not mean that an investor in an East German business would be burdened with the reduction of the workforce from the socialist to a market economy level. This adaptation typically was already carried out by the Treuhandanstalt when the business was privatised, although, depending on the investor's concept, further lay-offs may become necessary.

(e) Environmental Issues

Environmental issues tend to be a somewhat bigger problem in East Germany than in the west. The protection of the environment played no major role in the socialist economy. Environmental laws were frequently disregarded for political reasons. Pollution was also caused by the Soviet troops deployed on East German territory. Environmental issues basically may become relevant as liability for the contamination of real estate and with regard to the compliance of industrial facilities.

Under the statutory liability rules extended to East Germany, both the person who caused a contamination of land and the current owner of contaminated land may be held liable for clean-up. The risk of an investor associated with this situation is not as big as it may seem at first sight. First, it was possible during an interim period (which expired at the end of March 1992) to apply for an exemption from clean-up responsibility under public law, although such an exemption was not always granted and does not protect against third party liability towards neighbours. Second, the Treuhandanstalt usually undertook in its privatisation agreements to indemnify the purchaser against a substantial part of clean-up costs. Still, the best insurance against unexpected liability is an environmental audit if there is any chance of contamination.

The strict German environmental laws and licensing requirements now apply, in principle, also to facilities in East Germany. The outdated industrial equipment in East Germany usually does not comply with these standards. Facilities installed prior to July 1990 were in general "grandfathered" but they had to be brought to a state-of-the-art standard by the end of 1994 at the latest.

(f) **Bureaucracy**

Many state and local government agencies in East Germany are still being restructured. Understaffing may sometimes delay decisions on permits, investment priority decrees or registrations in real estate or commercial registers. On the other hand, the authorities are usually eager to support investments and will often facilitate the investor's way through bureaucracy.

(g) **Subsidies**

Substantial government subsidies and tax reliefs granted for investments in the Five New States have been an important incentive for investors. Most of the government programmes expired by the end of 1996 but some of them were extended.

(h) **Outlook**

None of the above-mentioned particularities should constitute an obstacle for an investment in Eastern Germany. Most acquisitions indeed have turned out to be quite successful. The costs of production are often still lower and economic growth in the coming years is expected to be substantially higher than in Western Germany. Reorganisations and the implementation of modern and sophisticated technology have enabled many businesses in the east to manufacture more efficiently and profitably than their counterparts in the west. The entire infrastructure of East Germany is being totally overhauled and may be superior in part to that in West Germany in the medium term. It is safe to say that East Germany holds a bright economic future and promises rewarding opportunities for investors, maybe more so than the western part of the country.

Index